CORNELIUS
NEPOS
·——— THREE LIVES ———·
ALCIBIADES • DION • ATTICUS

THE ALPHA CLASSICS

General Editor: R. C. CARRINGTON, M.A., D.Phil.

CAESAR'S GALLIC WAR, BOOK I, edited by C. Ewan, M.A.

CAESAR'S INVASIONS OF BRITAIN, edited by R. C. Carrington.

CICERO ON HIMSELF, selections from Cicero chosen and edited by N. Fullwood, B.A.

CORNELIUS NEPOS: THREE LIVES—ALCIBIADES, DION, ATTICUS, edited by R. Roebuck, M.A.

ERASMUS AND HIS TIMES, a selection from the Letters of Erasmus and his circle, edited by G. S. Facer, B.A.

HORACE ON HIMSELF, selections from Horace chosen and edited by A. H. Nash-Williams, M.A.

LIVY: BOOK V, edited by J. E. Pickstone, M.A.

LIVY: SCIPIO AFRICANUS, selections from Livy, Books XXVI-XXX, edited by T. A. Buckney, M.A.

LUCRETIUS ON MATTER AND MAN, edited by A. S. Cox, M.A.

MARTIAL AND HIS TIMES, selection from Martial, chosen and edited by K. W. D. Hull, M.A.

OVID ON HIMSELF, selections edited by J. A. Harrison, M.A.

OVID'S METAMORPHOSES: AN ANTHOLOGY, edited by J. E. Dunlop, M.A., Ph.D.

PLINY ON HIMSELF, selections from the Letters edited by H. A. B. White, M.A.

VERGIL'S AENEID I, edited by P. G. Hunter, M.A.

VERGIL'S AENEID II, edited by J. E. Dunlop, M.A., Ph.D.

VERGIL'S AENEID III, edited by R. W. Moore, M.A., D.Litt.

VERGIL'S AENEID IX, edited by B. Tilly, M.A., Ph.D.

VERGIL'S AENEID XII, edited by W. F. Gosling, M.A. and J. J. Smith, B.A.

Advanced Section

BEDE'S HISTORIA ECCLESIASTICA, a selection edited by F. W. Garforth, M.A.

LATIN PASTORALS—Vergil to Nemesianus, edited by J. E. Dunlop, M.A., Ph.D.

POEMS OF CATULLUS, edited by G. A. Williamson, M.A.

THE THOUGHT OF CICERO, selections from Cicero, edited by S. J. Wilson, B.A.

C O R N E L I U S
N E P O S
· ——— THREE LIVES ——— ·

ALCIBIADES • DION • ATTICUS

INTRODUCTION • TEXT • NOTES • VOCABULARY
BY

R. ROEBUCK M.A.

Published by
BRISTOL CLASSICAL PRESS (U.K.)
General Editor: John H. Betts
and
BOLCHAZY-CARDUCCI PUBLISHERS (U.S.A.)
(by arrangement with Bell & Hyman, Ltd.)
1987

© *Bell & Hyman, Ltd., 1958*

Reprinted, with permission, 1987, by

U.S.A.	*U.K.*
BOLCHAZY-CARDUCCI PUBLISHERS	*BRISTOL CLASSICAL PRESS*
44 Lake Street	*Department of Classics*
OAK PARK	*University of Bristol*
Illinois 60302	*Wills Memorial Building*
	Queens Road
	BRISTOL BS8 1RJ

ISBN 0-86516-207-7   *ISBN 0-86292-284-4*

Fourth Printing, 1987
Printed in the United States of America

PREFACE

Cornelius Nepos is regarded, with justification, as an easy author, and it is hoped that this book will provide beginners with an early means of escape from synthetic Latin. In the Notes an attempt has been made to give help both with the subject matter and with points of syntax and grammar which seem likely to present difficulty to an intelligent beginner. The Lives of Alcibiades, Dion and Atticus have been selected partly for their literary associations, partly to emphasise the continuity of the Greek and Roman worlds.

Besides such obvious works of reference as the Cambridge Ancient History, the editor wishes to express his indebtedness to E. F. Benson's *The Life of Alcibiades* and, in a different way to Carcopino's *Cicero: The Secrets of his Correspondence.* He must also thank the General Editor for his advice and for help with the Introduction.

The text used is that of the *Oxford Classical Texts* by kind permission of the Clarendon Press. For school use it has been thought advisable to make two small excisions.

R. R.

January, 1958

CONTENTS

INTRODUCTION   *page*

    I. The Author 1

    II. Historical Background . . . 3

TEXT

    ALCIBIADES 15

    DION 26

    ATTICUS 36

NOTES 57

INDEX OF PROPER NAMES . . . 101

VOCABULARY 109

LIST OF PLATES
(following page 2)

I. Piraeus (*Greek Information Office*)

II. Alcibiades (*Anderson*)

III. Athenian Tetradrachms (first two, *Bibliothèque National, Paris*; third, *British Museum*)

IV. (*a*) Socrates (*British Museum*); (*b*) Plato (*Anderson*)

V. Syracuse (*Foto-Stampa Angeli, Terni*)

VI. Coins from Asia Minor, Syracuse and Rome (*British Museum*)

VII. (*a*) Cicero (*Apsley House*); (*b*) Agrippa (*Alinari*)

VIII. The Appian Way (*E.N.I.T.*)

Map to illustrate the *Three Lives, pages* 12 and 13

INTRODUCTION

I THE AUTHOR

Very little information has come down to us about the personal history of Cornelius Nepos—even his name is not completely known. He was born about 100 B.C. in the North of Italy, possibly at Ticinum in the Po valley. Eventually, like other men of literary ability, he came to live at Rome, where he worked in close association with Atticus, a wealthy banker who had turned his attention to publishing. He outlived Atticus and died about 25 B.C.

What began, no doubt, as a strictly business relationship developed into friendship and we find Atticus, who was one of the most influential men in Rome, writing to commend Nepos to his other friends. The reaction of Cicero, at least, was distinctly cool. Even the news of the death of Nepos' son in 44 B.C. evokes from him only the most formal expression of sympathy, followed by the revealing admission that he did not know Nepos had a son. Another great literary figure, the poet Catullus, was more friendly. He dedicated a book of poems to Nepos and referred with approval to his industry as a historian.

The particular work which Catullus was praising, a *History of the World*, in three volumes, has not survived; nor have several mentioned by other writers. These include 'Lives' of Cicero and Cato, some love poems and a treatise on geography. What has survived is a number of 'Lives' from a work, *de Viris Illustribus*, which compared Romans and foreigners as generals, historians, poets, etc., leaving the reader to decide

I

who was best in these various categories. Of the twenty-five 'Lives,' twenty-two are of foreign generals, mostly Greek (including Alcibiades and Dion); one is a hotch-potch of various kings; and finally we have two (including Atticus) from the section on Roman historians.

Internal evidence shows that the work was originally published sometime before Atticus' death in 32 B.C. The last four chapters of the *Life of Atticus* were added, and possibly other changes made, in a second edition brought out probably before 27 B.C. (Nepos never refers to Octavian by the title Augustus which he received in that year.)

The work is of interest as the earliest example of biography in Latin which has survived. In its present fragmentary state it is obviously unbalanced; but, even when complete, it is difficult to imagine so varied a collection ever making up a satisfactory whole. Nor is its historical value very high, for important events in the lives of the men described are often briefly dismissed or even ignored. What Nepos is attempting is not a plain chronicle of facts. He wants to rouse his readers' interest by making the great names of History come alive as human beings: and in this, which is not the least of a biographer's duties, he has considerable success. The description, for example, of Alcibiades' return to Athens (VI, 3–5) conveys clearly the tremendous personality and strange fascination of the man; in the last chapters of Dion's 'Life' we share the dilemma of the philosopher turned tyrant in spite of himself; and, although we may be irritated at times by the aura of superhuman virtue which surrounds the portrait of Atticus, we can well understand Nepos' admiration for a kind-hearted man whose moral standards were far in advance of his day.

The language of the 'Lives' contains a number of archaisms, e.g. a preference for gerundives in -undus,

I. PIRAEUS, THE PORT OF ATHENS. This was already a busy place when Alcibiades arrived there in 406 B.C. on his return from exile (Alc. VI. 3). Five miles inland the Acropolis at Athens dominates the plain of Attica, crowned by the Parthenon, the temple which his guardian Pericles had lately built to honour the maiden goddess Athene.

II. ALCIBIADES. This bust by an unknown sculptor is now in the Vatican Museum, Rome.

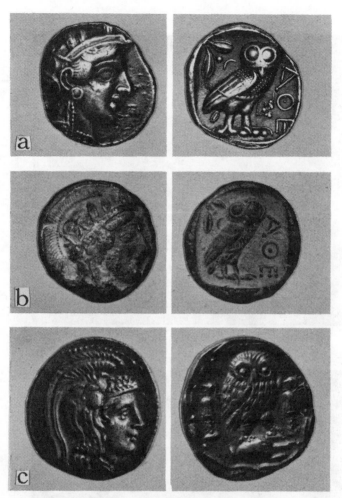

III. THREE ATHENIAN TETRADRACHMS. From 500 B.C. onwards Athenian coins bore the head of Athena, the city's patron goddess, and on the reverse her symbol the owl. The tetradrachm, or four drachma piece, was the largest silver coin in normal use. All three shown here differ slightly from the usual type.

(a) was minted in 411 by the Athenian fleet at Samos (see Alc. V. 3). It can be dated exactly by the small bull's head, a city emblem of Samos, which has been added above the owl's left foot.

(b) is of copper thinly coated with silver and was issued in 406 or shortly after, when the Athenian treasury had been exhausted by the Peloponnesian War. (Alc. VIII. I.)

(c) was minted by the Roman general Sulla in 87 B.C. after defeating Mithridates' forces (Att. IV. I-2). The trophies added on either side of the owl commemorate his victories at Chaeronea and Orchomenus, and were intended to humiliate Athens for her rash support of Mithridates.

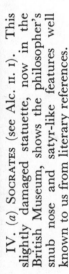

IV. (a) SOCRATES (see Alc. II. I). This slightly damaged statuette, now in the British Museum, shows the philosopher's snub nose and satyr-like features well known to us from literary references.

IV. (b) PLATO, the greatest of Socrates' pupils and a close friend of Dion (see Dion II and III). This bust is in the Vatican Museum. The eyes, now blank, were originally painted.

V. AN AERIAL VIEW OF MODERN SYRACUSE showing the 'Island' and parts of the two harbours. (See note Dion v. 5.)

VI. (*a*) Coin from Asia Minor with the head of a Persian governor, probably Tissaphernes (Alc. v. 2). On the reverse is a lyre and the Greek word *ΒΑΣΙΑ* meaning '(Persian) King'.

VI. (*b*) Syracusan Silver Decadrachm. This medallion is one of the finest examples of a type first struck to commemorate the Syracusan victory over the Athenian invaders in 413 B.C. and continued for at least another fifty years. This is a late version, possibly *c.* 360. Annual games were held in honour of the victory and the reverse shows a figure of Victory holding out a laurel wreath for the winner of the four-horse chariot race. Beneath are depicted captured Athenian arms and armour with the word *ΑΘΛΑ* (prizes). Contrast the muddle of the horses' legs with the highly successful composition of Arethusa's head and diving dolphins on the obverse.

VI. (*c*) Roman Denarius minted in Macedon by the republican leaders before their defeat at Philippi in 42 B.C. (Att. IX. 2). The obverse shows the head of Brutus, the reverse a cap of liberty, two daggers and EID MART (the day of Caesar's murder).

VII.   (a) CICERO.   The Apsley House bust gives an effective impression of Atticus' friend, the great orator who sought with little success to be also a man of action.

VII.   (b) AGRIPPA, the ablest general of Augustus and for some years son-in-law of Atticus.   This bust is in the Louvre, Paris.

VIII. THE APPIAN WAY.   This view was taken only four miles
from Rome.   Many of the basalt blocks have been removed and
the gaps are now filled with asphalt.   Ancient tombs can be seen
lining the road on either side.   (See Att. XXII. 4.)

and the style shows occasional rhetorical flourishes; but both are for the most part so straightforward that some critics have doubted whether the author could have been 'a learned contemporary of Cicero.' This, however, begs the question; and even though our manuscripts ascribe all but the last two 'Lives' to Aemilius Probus (late fourth century A.D.) there is no good reason for doubting that what we possess is the authentic work of Cornelius Nepos.

II Historical Background

At first sight the three men with whom we are here concerned appear to be scattered haphazardly across the history of the ancient world. Alcibiades was an Athenian who lived in the second half of the fifth century B.C.; a year or two after he was murdered Dion was born at Syracuse in Sicily; and 300 years later Atticus was born in Rome. Both in time and place they seem to have little in common: yet in a curious way there is one point where their different paths converge. Athens was Alcibiades' native city, and to Athens came both Dion and Atticus at a time of personal danger and found there the help and inspiration which this remarkable city has offered men for over 2000 years.

Athens

About 450 B.C., when Alcibiades was born, Athens was in every respect the most important city in Greece. Fifty years before she had been insignificant. Her victory, almost singlehanded, in 490 over the invading Persian army at Marathon had begun the transformation by giving the Athenians confidence in themselves. Ten years later their fleet, in which Themistocles had persuaded them to invest the profits from the State

silver mines, played a decisive part in defeating the
Persian navy at Salamis.   The same far-sighted
statesman then proceeded to organise a league among
various cities and islands of the Aegean to maintain a
navy for mutual defence against Persia.   By 450 this
organisation had turned into an Athenian empire, the
contributions of its members now paying for a fleet
whose primary function was to enforce their obedience
to the demands of Athens.

There is nothing very edifying or even unusual
about this acquisition of power.   Other states have
been victorious in other wars and risen to temporary
influence in the world.   What distinguishes the case
of Athens is the use she made of the income from her
empire.   Led by Pericles, the Athenian people began
to beautify their city with architecture and sculpture
which still in part survive and which have stirred the
awe and admiration of each succeeding generation.
If ever the end can justify the means, it did so here.
The Athenian empire, like other empires, may have
been morally wrong, but without it there would have
been no Parthenon.

The material prosperity of Athens we can understand; the exhilarating political climate of a genuine
democracy, where each citizen had an equal voice
and vote in state decisions, is something we can perhaps imagine; what remains a mystery is how Athens
in a single century could produce not only sculptors
and architects like Pheidias and Ictinus but also poets
and dramatists like Sophocles and Aristophanes, a
historian like Thucydides, and philosophers like
Socrates and Plato.   All these men of outstanding
genius were contemporaries of Alcibiades.   Most
of them would be known to him personally, for
Athens was not a large city and Pericles, in whose
home he was brought up, was not merely a statesman.
Profoundly interested in the ferment of ideas then

going on in Greece, he gathered round him the leading intellects of the Greek world, to discuss with them the new theories which were being formulated about art or music, about religion and science and, above all, about the nature and origins of the universe. It was in this stimulating atmosphere that Alcibiades grew up.

The outbreak of the Peloponnesian War in 431 was a turning point in the fortunes of Athens. Corinth was the prime instigator of the war. Her trade had declined as Athenian power had grown, and, fearing further losses, she incited her allies, who included Sparta, to demand that Athens should set the Greeks free. When the Athenians refused to disband their empire, a Peloponnesian army invaded Attica. The Long Walls connecting Athens with her harbour at the Piraeus prevented this and the succeeding annual invasions from being anything more than a nuisance. The Athenians retaliated with equally futile naval raids on the coast of the Peloponnese. Both operations, however, produced important accidental results. In 430 plague broke out at Athens, and because of serious overcrowding caused by the evacuation of Attica, it spread rapidly. In the end it wiped out a third of the population, a loss which was never made good. In 425 a chance landing at Pylos on the west coast of the Peloponnese enabled the Athenians to capture 294 Spartans. So desperately anxious was Sparta to get them back that in 421 when the two main advocates of continuing the war, Brasidas and Cleon, had een killed fighting one another in Thrace, peace was made at once.

But it was only a brief lull. Within two years fighting broke out again, for Sparta's allies still hoped for victory, and Alcibiades, who had now come to the fore at Athens, saw that his best way to power lay through war. He led the Athenians to believe that the quickest way to finish the war in Greece was by gaining control of the fabulous resources of Sicily. Fascinated by his oratory they approved his proposal for sending out an enormous expedition. They were soon disillusioned with the author of the scheme. When the original force proved inadequate a more prudent nation would have cut its losses. Instead the Athenians staked all they possessed to equip a second equally magnificent expedition. This also failed and ultimate defeat became only a question of time. That it took nine years and was not achieved without great help from Persia indicates both the resilience of the Athenians and the military genius of Alcibiades to whom in desperation they once more turned. After so much effort the end in 405 was ludicrous. At Aegospotami on the Hellespont Lysander captured 160 Athenian ships without resistance. Their crews had gone ashore to forage! Athens could do no more and surrendered.

Her worst fears were not in fact realised. Sparta resisted the demands of her allies for the total destruction of Athens and she emerged from her defeat weak and defenceless but still independent. For a short time she even seemed likely to build up a strong new league of maritime states—so grossly did the Spartans abuse their victory. But by 371 these dreams were abandoned for ever. Athens settled down to a new phase in her existence, which lacked the excitement of the previous century but brought its own satisfactions and achievements. With a reduced population and no foreign possessions the Athenians could still live in comparative comfort from their commerce. Fighting ceased to interest them. Even the eloquence of Demosthenes could scarcely rouse them against Philip of Macedon until it was too late. Yet they need not have disturbed themselves. From now on Athens was to find her past reputation sufficient protection against the new rulers of the world. Philip might destroy Thebes; later the Romans could burn Corinth to the ground; but even the ruthless Sulla, avenging her misguided support for Mithridates, shrank from the odium of inflicting a similar fate upon Athens.

Magna Graecia and Sicily

During the main period of Greek colonisation, from 750 to 600 B.C., a great number of settlers had established themselves along the east coast of Sicily and in southern Italy, especially around the Tarentine Gulf. So numerous were these Greek settlements in southern Italy that the area became known as Magna Graecia. Syracuse, founded from Corinth in 734, and Tarentum, from Sparta in 707, may be mentioned as perhaps the most important of the new towns.

Little is known of their early history. Clearly they had to struggle to maintain themselves against their barbarian neighbours and because of this ever present danger autocratic rule persisted in the west for more than a century after it had been superseded by democracy in Greece itself. The main danger came increasingly from the Carthaginians, who, from their base in North Africa, were seeking to extend their foothold in the west of Sicily. It can hardly have been a coincidence that Gelon, tyrant of Syracuse and the most powerful man in Sicily, was too busy resisting Carthaginian attacks to be able to help the Greeks in their struggle against Persia. There is a tradition that his victory at Himera in 480 occurred on the very day the Greeks defeated the Persian fleet at Salamis. Unlike the Persians, the Carthaginians were undeterred by their defeat. Continued pressure from the west meant continued tyranny for the Sicilian Greeks.

From time to time tyrants who became too oppressive were expelled and replaced for short periods by democracy. It was in one such interval that Syracuse repulsed the Athenian expeditions. Fresh encroachments by Carthage produced an atmosphere of nervousness, which in 405 enabled the elder Dionysius to seize power.

A man of humble birth, he possessed tremendous energy and courage. For a time he came to terms with Carthage, recognising her conquests and being recognised in return as ruler of Syracuse. Then, having turned the island of Ortygia into his private fortress, he began to enlarge Syracuse's territory at the expense of her Greek neighbours. Whole communities were sold as slaves for resisting his will: others were uprooted bodily and transferred to Syracuse. He pushed back the Carthaginians to the extreme west of Sicily, extended his empire into Italy and for a time became the strongest power in Europe. For close on forty years he ruled in splendour. He had the tyrant's traditional interest in the arts. He even wrote plays himself and submitted them for the annual festivals at Athens where one of them, *The Ransom of Hector*, gained first prize.

Despot though he was, his brother-in-law Dion found him a more tolerable master to serve than the son by whom he was succeeded in 367. This young man, Dionysius II, lacked his father's strength of character. He paid too much attention to unscrupulous advisers wishing to discredit the upright Dion. Finally he drove him into exile. Confusion returned once more to Sicily when Dion came back from Athens, drove out Dionysius and was himself assassinated three years later. Renewed Carthaginian pressure was held off with great difficulty until at last Rome arrived on the scene, defeated Carthage and turned Sicily into her first province (241 B.C.).

Rome

After acquiring Sicily, Rome proceeded to annex province after province until she had subdued all her rivals and gained control of the entire Mediterranean world. Even for Rome herself the process of expansion was not a comfortable one. The system of government by the Senate with the nominal consent of the People had worked well in the early days. Consuls and other annual magistrates had listened with respect to the collective wisdom of their fellow senators, and the rest of the State had acquiesced in their efficient rule.

Towards the end of the second century B.C. a change occurred. As Rome developed into a world power, the growth of wealth and luxury corrupted its ruling class. It could no longer be taken for granted that senators would be either competent or honest. Hence we find a number of reformers like the Gracchi attempting to govern in defiance of the Senate by appealing direct to the People, and thereby vastly increasing the bitterness of party politics at Rome. (The power of the popular assembly to pass laws without previous approval by the Senate had been granted in 287 but rarely exercised.) At the same time the problems of world government became too complex to be handled by governors sent out from Rome to govern a single province for a year. More and more power had to be entrusted to competent individuals like Sulla and Pompey, who sometimes used their armies to march on Rome and suppress their political opponents.

A particularly unpleasant period of violence occurred in 88–87. Sulla had marched on Rome and brutally murdered the tribune who was trying to deprive him of his command against Mithridates. No sooner had Sulla departed for the East than both

parties began to massacre their opponents indiscriminately.   It was to escape from this chaos that
Atticus decided to leave Rome.   On Sulla's return
there was further blood-letting, the notorious proscriptions of 81, in which nearly 5000 of his opponents,
including even senators, were cynically slaughtered.
Then as dictator he tried to strengthen the Senate by
imposing legal disabilities upon its potential rivals.
These measures, made possible only by his military
power, did not last.   The initiative in the State
passed inevitably to other military commanders,
first to Pompey the Great, then to Julius Caesar, a
still greater man.

Given the opportunity Caesar might well have
solved Rome's problems.   Some of his measures, for
example the inclusion of Gauls in the Senate, show
how enlightened was his approach.   But in Caesar's
time there still remained a few enthusiasts who
believed in the Republic.   They saw in him merely
a tyrant whose murder became a glorious, patriotic
duty.   Thirteen more years of civil war were needed
before the Romans as a nation were ready to forego
their liberties for the sake of peace and efficient
government.   Augustus, the heir of Caesar, gave them
both.   Small wonder that at the end of his long reign
his grateful subjects hailed him as a god.

Athens and Rome

It was no accident that Atticus should seek refuge
at Athens.   Rome first made contact with the
Greeks when her conquering armies entered Magna
Graecia early in the third century B.C.   The yeoman
farmers who defeated Pyrrhus were introduced to a
new and exciting civilisation.   The Greeks had much
to teach: the best of the Romans were very willing to
learn. Greek architecture, literature, oratory and

drama roused their interest.   Greek slaves like Livius
Andronicus were found to translate Homer's *Odyssey*
and other great works into Latin.   Presently it
was recognised that the true centre of Greek civilisation lay beyond Magna Graecia, and interest shifted
to Athens.

Students had been coming to Athens from far and
near ever since 387 when Plato on his return from his
first visit to Syracuse established a college in a wood-
land grove, Academia, near Athens.   Here mathe-
matics and philosophy were to be studied by selected
students, following the principles which Plato had
learnt from Socrates.   The Academy, as the college
came to be called, marks the beginning of higher
education as we know it.   Few of its pupils attained
the eminence of Aristotle who came in 367 at the age
of seventeen and stayed for twenty years, but from the
outset it never lacked distinguished scholars.   Other
establishments of a similar nature, Aristotle's Lyceum
for one, were subsequently set up in Athens which
developed into a quiet and supremely beautiful
university city.   Dion in exile was one of the first to
shelter there.   Atticus three centuries later was not
by any means the last.   By his day it was the custom
for young Romans, whose families could afford it, to
complete their education by spending two or three
years abroad, preferably at Athens, in much the same
way as young English noblemen in the eighteenth
century made the Grand Tour of Europe.   That was
no doubt Atticus' original intention, for he was only
twenty-one when his stay began.   Among other
Romans who went to Athens to study, the poet Horace
may be mentioned as well as Atticus' nephew, young
Quintus Cicero, and young Marcus Cicero, the orator's
son.

For hundreds of years men came, seeking education
and taking away a deepened understanding of what

B

River Tiber

I T A L Y

ADRIATIC SEA

Nomentum
Rome
Via Appia

Capua
Via Appia
Brundisium
Tarentum

M A

E P I

Thurii
Corcyra

Zacynthus

S I C I L Y
Heraclea
Minoa
Syracuse

N

0 20 40 60 80 100 120 140 160 180 200 Miles

the Greek genius had achieved.   'Conquered Greece',
wrote Horace, 'took her fierce conqueror captive'.
Great is our debt to Rome for respecting and preserv-
ing the heritage of Greece: infinitely greater our debt
to Athens, which in her exuberant youth created that
heritage, and in tranquil old age imparted it to Rome
and through her to the world.

CORNELIUS NEPOS: THREE LIVES

ALCIBIADES

c. 450–404 B.C.

The career of Alcibiades is the story of a man who had every advantage of birth and upbringing. He was blessed in addition with wit, intelligence, good looks and quite irresistible charm. Yet in spite of all this—or perhaps because of it—he never developed a sense of responsibility, or the moral strength which is needed for greatness.

As a boy he was inevitably spoilt by admiring friends and relations. Pericles, the great statesman who was his guardian, made little impression. But Socrates, who loved him not for his physical beauty but for the potential beauty of his soul, was a powerful influence for good, which persisted at least until Alcibiades was twenty-seven. From then on, vanity and a craving for the spectacular dominated his life, causing immeasurable harm to Athens.

Having quickly wrecked the Peace of Nicias which might have ended the Peloponnesian War, he set his fellow countrymen hankering after the Sicilian adventure from whose failure they never recovered. (Not that he should be blamed too harshly for this. Given the chance, he might even have brought it to a successful conclusion.) From Sparta out of sheer vindictiveness he dealt Athens two crippling blows, knowing her weaknesses more clearly than his hosts. From Sardis, where he fled after making Sparta too hot to hold him, his intrigues played no small part in the mercifully short-lived oligarchic revolution of 411.

Yet the restored democracy at Athens was still ready to forgive and forget; and in 407 gave him sole command of its forces. Even in 405, after he had forsaken her for the second time, we find that Athens 'misses him, but hates him, yet longs to have him back' (Aristophanes *Frogs* 1425).

His lonely and pathetic death was a fitting end to the tragedy of a man who could inspire such vast and undeserved devotion.

I

CH I.   *The remarkable contradictions in Alcibiades' character suggest an experiment by Nature to see what she could produce.*

Alcibiades, Cliniae filius, Atheniensis. in hoc quid natura efficere possit videtur experta. constat enim inter omnes, qui de eo memoriae prodiderunt, nihil illo fuisse excellentius vel in vitiis vel in virtutibus. 2 natus in amplissima civitate summo genere, omnium aetatis suae multo formosissimus; ad omnes res aptus consiliique plenus (namque imperator fuit summus et mari et terra); disertus, ut in primis dicendo valeret, quod tanta erat commendatio oris atque orationis, ut nemo ei [dicendo] posset resistere; dives; / cum 3 tempus posceret, laboriosus, patiens; liberalis, splendidus non minus in vita quam victu; affabilis, 4 blandus, temporibus callidissime serviens: idem, simul ac se remiserat neque causa suberat quare animi laborem perferret, luxuriosus, dissolutus, libidinosus, intemperans reperiebatur, ut omnes admirarentur in uno homine tantam esse dissimilitudinem tamque diversam naturam.

II

CH. 2. *He was fortunate both in his upbringing and in his wealthy marriage. Socrates was among his many admirers.*

Educatus est in domo Pericli (privignus enim eius fuisse dicitur), eruditus a Socrate. socerum habuit Hipponicum, omnium Graeca lingua loquentium ditissimum, ut, si ipse fingere vellet, neque plura bona reminisci neque maiora posset consequi, quam vel natura vel fortuna tribueret. . . .

III

CH. 3. *He was chosen by the Athenians as joint commander of their Sicilian Expedition (415). Before its departure the statues of Hermes were mutilated and many suspected Alcibiades.*

Bello Peloponnesio huius consilio atque auctoritate Athenienses bellum Syracusanis indixerunt: ad quod gerendum ipse dux delectus est, duo praeterea collegae dati, Nicia et Lamachus. id cum appararetur, 2 prius quam classis exiret, accidit ut una nocte omnes Hermae, qui in oppido erant Athenis, deicerentur praeter unum, qui ante ianuam erat Andocidi (itaque ille postea Mercurius Andocidi vocitatus est). hoc 3 cum appareret non sine magna multorum consensione esse factum, quae non ad privatam, sed publicam rem pertineret, magnus multitudini timor est iniectus, ne qua repentina vis in civitate exsisteret, quae libertatem opprimeret populi. hoc maxime convenire in Alci- 4 biadem videbatur, quod et potentior et maior quam privatus existimabatur: multos enim liberalitate devinxerat, plures etiam opera forensi suos reddiderat.

5 qua re fiebat ut omnium oculos, quotienscumque in
publicum prodisset, ad se converteret neque ei par
quisquam in civitate poneretur. itaque non solum
spem in eo habebant maximam, sed etiam timorem,
6 quod et obesse plurimum et prodesse poterat. asper-
gebatur etiam infamia, quod in domo sua facere
mysteria dicebatur (quod nefas erat more Atheniensium) idque non ad religionem, sed ad coniurationem
pertinere existimabatur.

IV

CH. 4. *When recalled from Sicily for trial he went instead*
to Sparta, which was at war with Athens. His advice to
the Spartans was very harmful to Athens.

Hoc crimine in contione ab inimicis compellabatur.
sed instabat tempus ad bellum proficiscendi. id ille
intuens neque ignorans civium suorum consuetudinem
postulabat, si quid de se agi vellent, potius de praesente quaestio haberetur, quam absens invidiae
2 crimine accusaretur. inimici vero eius quiescendum
in praesenti, quia noceri non posse intellegebant, et
illud tempus exspectandum decreverunt, quo is exisset,
3 ut absentem aggrederentur. itaque fecerunt. nam
postquam in Siciliam eum pervenisse crediderunt,
absentem, quod sacra violasset, reum fecerunt. qua
de re cum ei nuntius a magistratu in Siciliam missus
esset, ut domum ad causam dicendam rediret, essetque
in magna spe provinciae bene administrandae, non
parere noluit et in trierem, quae ad eum erat deport-
4 andum missa, ascendit. hac Thurios in Italiam
pervectus, multa secum reputans de immoderata
civium suorum licentia crudelitateque erga nobiles,

utilissimum ratus impendentem evitare tempestatem, clam se ab custodibus subduxit et inde primum Elidem, dein Thebas venit. postquam autem se 5 capitis damnatum bonis publicatis audivit, et, id quod usu venerat, Eumolpidas sacerdotes a populo coactos ut se devoverent, eiusque devotionis quo testatior esset memoria, exemplum in pila lapidea incisum esse positum in publico, Lacedaemonem demigravit. ibi, 6 ut ipse praedicare consuerat, non adversus patriam, sed inimicos suos bellum gessit, quod eidem hostes essent civitati: nam cum intellegerent se plurimum prodesse posse rei publicae, ex ea eiecisse plusque irae suae quam utilitati communi paruisse. itaque huius 7 consilio Lacedaemonii cum Perse rege amicitiam fecerunt, dein Deceleam in Attica munierunt praesidioque ibi perpetuo posito in obsidione Athenas tenuerunt. eiusdem opera Ioniam a societate averterunt Atheniensium. quo facto multo superiores bello esse coeperunt.

V

CH. 5. *Realising the Spartans did not trust him, he moved to Sardis (412) and won the confidence of the Persian governor Tissaphernes. He was invited to command the Athenian fleet at Samos, and gained important successes against the Spartans in Ionia and the Hellespont (411–408).*

Neque vero his rebus tam amici Alcibiadi sunt facti quam timore ab eo alienati. nam cum acerrimi viri praestantem prudentiam in omnibus rebus cognoscerent, pertimuerunt ne caritate patriae ductus aliquando ab ipsis desciscerent et cum suis in gratiam rediret. itaque tempus eius interficiundi quaerere instituerunt. id Alcibiades diutius celari non potuit: 2

erat enim ea sagacitate, ut decipi non posset, praesertim cum animum attendisset ad cavendum.   itaque ad Tissaphernem, praefectum regis Darii, se
3 contulit.   cuius cum in intimam amicitiam pervenisset
et Atheniensium male gestis in Sicilia rebus opes
senescere, contra Lacedaemoniorum crescere videret,
initio cum Pisandro praetore, qui apud Samum exercitum habebat, per internuntios colloquitur et de
reditu suo facit mentionem.   erat enim eodem quo
Alcibiades sensu, populi potentiae non amicus et
4 optimatium fautor.   ab hoc destitutus primum per
Thrasybulum, Lyci filium, ab exercitu recipitur
praetorque fit apud Samum, post suffragante Theramene populi scito restituitur parique absens imperio
praeficitur simul cum Thrasybulo et Theramene.
5 horum in imperio tanta commutatio rerum facta est,
ut Lacedaemonii, qui paulo ante victores viguerant,
perterriti pacem peterent. victi enim erant quinque
proeliis terrestribus, tribus navalibus, in quibus
ducentas naves triremes amiserant, quae captae in
6 hostium venerant potestatem.   Alcibiades simul cum
collegis receperat Ioniam, Hellespontum, multas
praeterea urbes Graecas, quae in ora sitae sunt Asiae
quarum expugnarant complures, in his Byzantium,
neque minus multas consilio ad amicitiam adiun-
7 xerant, quod in captos clementia fuerant usi.   ita
praeda onusti, locupletato exercitu, maximis rebus
gestis Athenas venerunt.

VI

CH. 6.   *On his return to Athens* (407) *he was received
with wild enthusiasm.*

His cum obviam universa civitas in Piraeum des-
cendisset, tanta fuit omnium exspectatio visendi

Alcibiadis, ut ad eius triremem vulgus conflueret, proinde ac si solus advenisset. sic enim populo erat 2 persuasum, et adversas superiores et praesentes secundas res accidisse eius opera. itaque et Siciliae amissum et Lacedaemoniorum victorias culpae suae tribuebant, quod talem virum e civitate expulissent. neque id sine causa arbitrari videbantur. nam postquam exercitui praeesse coeperat, neque terra neque mari hostes pares esse potuerant. hic ut e navi 3 egressus est, quamquam Theramenes et Thrasybulus eisdem rebus praefuerant simulque venerant in Piraeum, tamen unum omnes illum prosequebantur, et, id quod numquam antea usu venerat nisi Olympiae victoribus, coronis aureis aeneisque vulgo donabatur. ille lacrumans talem benivolentiam civium suorum accipiebat, reminiscens pristini temporis acerbitatem. postquam astu venit, contione advo- 4 cata sic verba fecit, ut nemo tam ferus fuerit, quin eius casum lacrumarit inimicumque iis se ostenderit, quorum opera patria pulsus fuerat, proinde ac si alius populus, non ille ipse qui tum flebat, eum sacrilegii damnasset. restituta ergo huic sunt publice bona, 5 eidemque illi Eumolpidae sacerdotes rursus resacrare sunt coacti, qui eum devoverant, pilaeque illae, in quibus devotio fuerat scripta, in mare praecipitatae.

VII

CH. 7. *He was appointed sole commander. A minor reverse (406) broke the spell and Alcibiades was not elected general for 405. He withdrew to the Thracian Chersonese.*

Haec Alcibiadi laetitia non nimis fuit diuturna. nam cum ei omnes essent honores decreti totaque res

publica domi bellique tradita, ut unius arbitrio
gereretur, et ipse postulasset ut duo sibi collegae
darentur, Thrasybulus et Adimantus, neque id nega-
tum esset, classe in Asiam profectus, quod apud
Cymen minus ex sententia rem gesserat, in invidiam
recidit: nihil enim eum non efficere posse ducebant.

2 ex quo fiebat ut omnia minus prospere gesta culpae
tribuerent, cum aut eum neglegenter aut malitiose
fecisse loquerentur, sicut tum accidit: nam corrup-

3 tum a rege capere Cymen noluisse arguebant.   itaque
huic maxime putamus malo fuisse nimiam opinionem
ingenii atque virtutis: timebatur enim non minus
quam diligebatur, ne secunda fortuna magnisque
opibus elatus tyrannidem concupisceret. quibus
rebus factum est ut absenti magistratum abrogarent

4 et alium in eius locum substituerent.   id ille ut audivit, domum reverti noluit et se Pactyen contulit ibique
tria castella communiit, Ornos, Bizanthen, Neontichos, manuque collecta primus Graecae civitatis in
Threciam introiit, gloriosius existimans barbarum

5 praeda locupletari quam Graiorum.   qua ex re cre-
verat cum fama tum opibus, magnamque amicitiam
sibi cum quibusdam regibus Threciae pepererat.

VIII

CH. 8.   *His good advice did not save the Athenian fleet at*
Aegospotami and Athens had to surrender to Lysander (404).

Neque tamen a caritate patriae potuit recedere.
nam cum apud Aegos flumen Philocles, praetor
Atheniensium, classem constituisset suam neque longe
abesset Lysander, praetor Lacedaemoniorum, qui in
eo erat occupatus ut bellum quam diutissime duceret,

quod ipsis pecunia a rege suppeditabatur, contra
Atheniensibus exhaustis praeter arma et naves nihil
erat super, Alcibiades ad exercitum venit Athenien- 2
sium ibique praesente vulgo agere coepit: si vellent,
se coacturum Lysandrum dimicare aut pacem petere
spopondit; Lacedaemonios eo nolle classe confligere,
quod pedestribus copiis plus quam navibus valerent;
sibi autem esse facile Seuthem, regem Threcum, 3
deducere ut eum terra depelleret: quo facto neces-
sario aut classe conflicturum aut bellum composi-
turum. id etsi vere dictum Philocles animadvertebat, 4
tamen postulata facere noluit, quod sentiebat se
Alcibiade recepto nullius momenti apud exercitum
futurum et, si quid secundi evenisset, nullam in ea re
suam partem fore, contra ea, si quid adversi accidisset,
se unum eius delicti futurum reum. ab hoc discedens 5
Alcibiades 'quoniam' inquit 'victoriae patriae repug-
nas, illud moneo, *ne* iuxta hostem castra habeas
nautica: periculum est enim, ne immodestia militum
vestrorum occasio detur Lysandro vestri opprimendi
exercitus.' neque ea res illum fefellit. nam Ly- 6
sander, cum per speculatores comperisset vulgum
Atheniensium in terram praedatum exisse navesque
paene inanes relictas, tempus rei gerendae non dimisit
eoque impetu bellum totum delevit.

IX

CH. 9. *Feeling unsafe even in Thrace, Alcibiades ap-
proached Pharnabazus, the Persian governor of Phrygia and
won his confidence.*

At Alcibiades, victis Atheniensibus non satis tuta
eadem loca sibi arbitrans, penitus in Threciam se
supra Propontidem abdidit, sperans ibi facillime

2 suam fortunam occuli posse. falso. nam Threces,
postquam eum cum magna pecunia venisse senserunt,
insidias fecerunt: qui ea quae apportarat abstulerunt,
3 ipsum capere non potuerunt. ille cernens nullum
locum sibi tutum in Graecia propter potentiam Lacedaemoniorum ad Pharnabazum in Asiam transiit,
quem quidem adeo sua cepit humanitate, ut eum
nemo in amicitia antecederet. namque ei Grynium
dederat, in Phrygia castrum, ex quo quinquagena
4 talenta vectigalis capiebat. qua fortuna Alcibiades
non erat contentus neque Athenas victas Lacedaemoniis servire poterat pati. itaque ad patriam
5 liberandam omni ferebatur cogitatione. sed videbat
id sine rege Perse non posse fieri, ideoque eum amicum
sibi cupiebat adiungi neque dubitabat facile se consecuturum, si modo eius conveniundi habuisset
potestatem. nam Cyrum fratrem ei bellum clam
parare Lacedaemoniis adiuvantibus sciebat: id si
aperuisset, magnam se initurum gratiam videbat.

X

CH. 10.   *He was planning to gain for Athens the support
of the new Persian king, when Pharnabazus, under pressure
from Lysander, gave orders for his murder.   With difficulty
these orders were carried out (404).*

Hoc cum moliretur peteretque a Pharnabazo, ut
ad regem mitteretur, eodem tempore Critias ceterique
tyranni Atheniensium certos homines ad Lysandrum
in Asiam miserant, qui eum certiorem facerent, nisi
Alcibiadem sustulisset, nihil earum rerum fore ratum,
quas ipse Athenis constituisset: quare, si suas res
2 gestas manere vellet, illum persequeretur. his Laco

rebus commotus statuit accuratius sibi agendum cum
Pharnabazo. huic ergo renuntiat quae regi cum
Lacedaemoniis essent, nisi Alcibiadem vivum aut
mortuum sibi tradidisset. non tulit hunc satrapes et 3
violare clementiam quam regis opes minui maluit.
itaque misit Susamithren et Bagaeum ad Alcibiadem
interficiendum, cum ille esset in Phrygia iterque ad
regem compararet. missi clam vicinitati, in qua tum 4
Alcibiades erat, dant negotium ut eum interficiant.
illi cum ferro aggredi non auderent, noctu ligna
contulerunt circa casam eam, in qua quiescebat,
eamque succenderunt, ut incendio conficerent, quem
manu superari posse diffidebant. ille autem ut 5
sonitu flammae est excitatus, etsi gladius ei erat sub-
ductus, familiaris sui subalare telum eripuit. namque erat cum eo quidam ex Arcadia hospes, qui
numquam discedere voluerat. hunc sequi se iubet et
id quod in praesentia vestimentorum fuit arripit.
his in ignem eiectis flammae vim transiit. quem ut 6
barbari incendium effugisse viderunt, telis eminus
missis interfecerunt caputque eius ad Pharnabazum
rettulerunt. at mulier, quae cum eo vivere consuerat,
muliebri sua veste contectum aedificii incendio mortuum cremavit, quod ad vivum interimendum erat
comparatum. sic Alcibiades annos circiter XL natus
diem obiit supremum.

XI

CH. 11. *The verdict of three eminent historians: Alcibiades' versatility and charm made him outstanding amongst
Greeks, Thracians and Persians alike.*

Hunc infamatum a plerisque tres gravissimi historici summis laudibus extulerunt: Thucydides, qui

eiusdem aetatis fuit, Theopompus, post aliquanto natus, et Timaeus: qui quidem duo maledicentissimi nescio quo modo in illo uno laudando consenserunt.

2 namque ea, quae supra scripsimus, de eo praedicarunt atque hoc amplius: cum Athenis, splendidissima civitate, natus esset, omnes splendore ac dignitate

3 superasse vitae; postquam inde expulsus Thebas venerit, adeo studiis eorum inservisse, ut nemo eum labore corporisque viribus posset aequiperare (omnes enim Boeotii magis firmitati corporis quam ingenii

4 acumini inserviunt); eundem apud Lacedaemonios, quorum moribus summa virtus in patientia ponebatur, sic duritiae se dedisse, ut parsimonia victus atque cultus omnes Lacedaemonios vinceret; fuisse apud Thracas, homines vinolentos rebusque veneriis

5 deditos: hos quoque in his rebus antecessisse; venisse ad Persas, apud quos summa laus esset fortiter venari, luxuriose vivere: horum sic imitatum consuetudinem,

6 ut illi ipsi eum in his maxime admirarentur. quibus rebus effecisse ut, apud quoscumque esset, princeps poneretur habereturque carissimus. sed satis de hoc: reliquos ordiamur.

DION

c. 408–353 B.C.

Dion was a humane and talented man, who did what he could to mitigate the excesses of the two rulers of Syracuse in whose reigns he lived; but if he had not met the Athenian philosopher Plato, it is unlikely he would ever have made a name for himself.

Plato had observed the fickle and often cruel behaviour of democracy at Athens under the strain of a long war. When it condemned his master Socrates to death he had been finally disgusted and decided that the only hope of good government lay in a philosopher-king. (*See* Plato, *Republic*, Bk. V, 473 D.) Such a ruler, knowing by training and intuition what courses were best for his country, would govern reluctantly, driven to do so by the knowledge that otherwise the job must be done less well by other men, and that he himself and his country would suffer. His fellow citizens, it was hoped, would recognise what was best for them and accept his rule.

Plato and Dion first met in 387 when the philosopher, on a visit to Tarentum in southern Italy, accepted a pressing invitation from the elder Dionysius to come to Syracuse. It was Dion who had instigated the invitation. Plato, though making no secret of his loathing for tyrants, was obliged to respect the achievements of a man who had made Syracuse the strongest power in the Mediterranean at that time. When Dionysius died in 367, it seems to have occurred to both Plato and Dion that his son, the younger Dionysius, who had succeeded to the throne, provided an opportunity for experimenting in the production of a philosopher-king. Plato at once sailed for Syracuse. The experiment, in spite of a promising beginning, failed. Dion was exiled and Plato shortly afterwards left for Athens.

In exile Dion resolved to remove an unworthy ruler. His unexpectedly rapid success when he landed in Sicily in 357 presented him with the chance to take the part of philosopher-king himself; and to this he clung although all the Syracusans wanted from him was the restoration of their democracy. The explanation given by Nepos for Dion's growing unpopularity is scarcely credible. His obstinate

c

retention of power had become reason enough for his violent removal. Here again we have tragedy—in the best traditions of Greek drama.

It should be noted that Nepos' account of Dion's last years differs substantially from the fuller versions of our other authorities, Diodorus and Plutarch, who indicate no departure from his earlier austere standards of conduct.

I

CH. 1. *Dion was related by marriage both to Dionysius I of Syracuse and to his son. He was especially intimate with the elder Dionysius who employed him on many important embassies.*

Dion, Hipparini filius, Syracusanus, nobili genere natus, utraque implicatus tyrannide Dionysiorum. namque ille superior Aristomachen, sororem Dionis, habuit in matrimonio, ex qua duos filios, Hipparinum et Nisaeum, procreavit totidemque filias, nomine Sophrosynen et Areten, quarum priorem Dionysio filio, eidem cui regnum reliquit, nuptum dedit, alter-
2 am, Areten, Dioni. Dion autem praeter nobilem propinquitatem generosamque maiorum famam multa alia ab natura habuit bona, in his ingenium docile, come, aptum ad artes optimas, magnam corporis dignitatem, quae non minimum commendat, magnas praeterea divitias a patre relictas, quas ipse
3 tyranni muneribus auxerat. erat intimus Dionysio priori, neque minus propter mores quam affinitatem. namque etsi Dionysii crudelitas ei displicebat, tamen salvum propter necessitudinem, magis etiam suorum causa studebat. aderat in magnis rebus, eiusque consilio multum movebatur tyrannus, nisi qua in re

maior ipsius cupiditas intercesserat. legationes vero 4
omnes, quae essent illustriores, per Dionem adminis-
trabantur: quas quidem ille diligenter obeundo,
fideliter administrando crudelissimum nomen tyranni
sua humanitate leniebat. hunc a Dionysio missum 5
Karthaginienses suspexerunt, ut neminem umquam
Graeca lingua loquentem magis sint admirati.

II

Ch. 2.   *Having persuaded Dionysius I to invite Plato to
Syracuse*, (387 b.c.) *he became a devoted admirer of the
philosopher. Distrusting Dion, the younger Dionysius
hastened his father's death* (367).

Neque vero haec Dionysium fugiebant: nam
quanto esset sibi ornamento, sentiebat. quo fiebat ut
uni huic maxime indulgeret neque eum secus diligeret
ac filium: qui quidem, cum Platonem Tarentum 2
venisse fama in Siciliam esset perlata, adulescenti
negare non potuerit, quin eum accerseret, cum Dion
eius audiendi cupiditate flagraret. dedit ergo huic
veniam magnaque eum ambitione Syracusas perduxit. quem Dion adeo admiratus est atque 3
adamavit, ut se ei totum traderet. neque vero minus
ipse Plato delectatus est Dione. itaque cum a Dionysio
crudeliter violatus esset, quippe quem venumdari
iussisset, tamen eodem rediit eiusdem Dionis precibus
adductus. interim in morbum incidit Dionysius. 4
quo cum gravi conflictaretur, quaesivit a medicis
Dion, quem ad modum se haberet, simulque ab iis
petiit, si forte maiori esset periculo, ut sibi faterentur:
nam velle se cum eo colloqui de partiendo regno,
quod sororis suae filios ex illo natos partem regni

5 putabat debere habere. id medici non tacuerunt et
ad Dionysium filium sermonem rettulerunt. quo ille
commotus, ne agendi esset Dioni potestas, patri
soporem medicos dare coegit. hoc aeger sumpto ut
somno sopitus diem obiit supremum.

III

Cн. 3. *For a time the feud was concealed. With
Dionysius' consent Dion invited Plato for a second visit* (367)*;
but the historian Philistus, lately restored from exile,
counteracted Plato's liberalising influence.*

Tale initium fuit Dionis et Dionysii simultatis,
eaque multis rebus aucta est. sed tamen primis
temporibus aliquamdiu simulata inter eos amicitia
mansit. cum Dion non desisteret obsecrare Dionysium, ut Platonem Athenis arcesseret et eius consiliis
uteretur, ille, qui in aliqua re vellet patrem imitari,
2 morem ei gessit. eodemque tempore Philistum his-
toricum Syracusas reduxit, hominem amicum non
magis tyranno quam tyrannis. sed de hoc in eo libro
plura sunt exposita, qui de historicis Graecis conscrip-
3 tus est. Plato autem tantum apud Dionysium auctoritate potuit valuitque eloquentia, ut ei persuaserit
tyrannidis facere finem libertatemque reddere Syracusanis. a qua voluntate Philisti consilio deterritus
aliquanto crudelior esse coepit.

IV

Cн. 4. *Overcome by his jealousy the tyrant now banished
Dion to Corinth* (366)*, compelled his wife to marry again,
and corrupted his son.*

Qui quidem cum a Dione se superari videret in-
genio, auctoritate, amore populi, verens ne, si eum
secum haberet, aliquam occasionem sui daret opprimendi, navem ei trireniem dedit, qua Corinthum
deveheretur, ostendens se id utriusque facere causa,
ne, cum inter se timerent, alteruter alterum prae-
occuparet. id cum factum multi indignarentur 2
magnaeque esset invidiae tyranno, Dionysius omnia,
quae moveri poterant Dionis, in navis imposuit ad
eumque misit. sic enim existimari volebat, id se non
odio hominis, sed suae salutis fecisse causa. postea 3
vero quam audivit eum in Peloponneso manum com-
parare sibique bellum facere conari, Areten, Dionis
uxorem, alii nuptum dedit filiumque eius sic educari
iussit, ut indulgendo turpissimis imbueretur cupidi-
tatibus. nam . . . vino epulisque obruebatur, neque 4
ullum tempus sobrio relinquebatur. is usque eo 5
vitae statum commutatum ferre non potuit, postquam
in patriam rediit pater (namque appositi erant custodes, qui eum a pristino victu deducerent), ut se de
superiore parte aedium deiecerit atque ita interierit.
sed illuc revertor.

V

CH. 5. *In Corinth Dion and a fellow exile, Heraclides,
found few to support what seemed a hopeless cause. Returning at last (357) with only two merchant ships, Dion
was immediately successful. Dionysius withdrew to Italy.*

Postquam Corinthum pervenit Dion et eodem per-
fugit Heraclides ab eodem expulsus Dionysio, qui
praefectus fuerat equitum, omni ratione bellum com-
parare coeperunt. sed non multum proficiebant, 2

quod multorum annorum tyrannus magnarum opum
putabatur: quam ob causam pauci ad societatem
3 periculi perducebantur. sed Dion, fretus non tam
suis copiis quam odio tyranni, maximo animo duabus
onerariis navibus quinquaginta annorum imperium,
munitum quingentis longis navibus, decem equitum
centumque peditum milibus, profectus oppugnatum,
quod omnibus gentibus admirabile est visum, adeo
facile perculit, ut post diem tertium, quam Siciliam
attigerat, Syracusas introierit. ex quo intellegi
potest nullum esse imperium tutum nisi benevolentia
4 munitum. eo tempore aberat Dionysius et in Italia
classem opperiebatur adversariorum, ratus neminem
sine magnis copiis ad se venturum. quae res eum
5 fefellit. nam Dion iis ipsis, qui sub adversarii fuerant
potestate, regios spiritus repressit totiusque eius partis
Siciliae potitus est, quae sub Dionysii fuerat potestate,
parique modo urbis Syracusarum praeter arcem et
insulam adiunctam oppido, eoque rem perduxit, ut
6 talibus pactionibus pacem tyrannus facere vellet:
Siciliam Dion obtineret, Italiam Dionysius, Syracusas
Apollocrates, cui maximam fidem uni habebat Dion.

VI

CH. 6.   *Dion's luck did not last.   His son's suicide was
followed by quarrels with Heraclides.   Having resolved to
share his power with nobody, he had Heraclides murdered.*

Has tam prosperas tamque inopinatas res consecuta
est subita commutatio, quod fortuna sua mobilitate,
quem paulo ante extulerat, demergere est adorta.
2 primum in filio, de quo commemoravi supra, suam
vim exercuit. nam cum uxorem reduxisset, quae alii

fuerat tradita, filiumque vellet revocare ad virtutem
a perdita luxuria, accepit gravissimum parens vulnus
morte filii. deinde orta dissensio est inter eum et 3
Heraclidem, qui, quod ei principatum non concedebat,
factionem comparavit. neque is minus valebat apud
optimates, quorum consensu praeerat classi, cum Dion
exercitum pedestrem teneret. non tulit hoc animo 4
aequo Dion, et versum illum Homeri rettulit ex
secunda rhapsodia, in quo haec sententia est: non
posse bene geri rem publicam multorum imperiis. quod
dictum magna invidia consecuta est: namque aperuisse
videbatur omnia in sua potestate esse velle. hanc
ille non lenire obsequio, sed acerbitate opprimere 5
studuit, Heraclidemque, cum Syracusas venisset,
interficiundum curavit.

VII

Сн. 7. *In order to pay his mercenaries Dion was obliged
to plunder first his enemies, then his friends. His consequent
unpopularity grieved him.*

Quod factum omnibus maximum timorem iniecit:
nemo enim illo interfecto se tutum putabat. ille
autem adversario remoto licentius eorum bona, quos
sciebat adversus se sensisse, militibus dispertivit.
quibus divisis cum cotidiani maximi fierent sumptus, 2
celeriter pecunia deesse coepit, neque, quo manus
porrigeret, suppetebat nisi in amicorum possessiones.
id eius modi erat, ut, cum milites reconciliasset,
amitteret optimates. quarum rerum cura frange- 3
batur et insuetus male audiendi non animo aequo
ferebat, de se ab iis male existimari, quorum paulo

ante in caelum fuerat elatus laudibus.   vulgus autem offensa in eum militum voluntate liberius loquebatur et tyrannum non ferendum dictitabat.

VIII

CH. 8.   *A false friend, Callicrates, intrigued against him. Though warned by his wife and sister, Dion did not realise his danger.*

Haec ille intuens cum quem ad modum sedaret nesciret et quorsum evaderent timeret, Callicrates quidam, civis Atheniensis, qui simul cum eo ex Peloponneso in Siciliam venerat, homo et callidus et ad fraudem acutus, sine ulla religione ac fide, adit ad
2 Dionem et ait: eum magno in periculo esse propter offensionem populi et odium militum, quod nullo modo evitare posset, nisi alicui suorum negotium daret, qui se simularet illi inimicum. quem si invenisset idoneum, facile omnium animos cogniturum adversariosque sublaturum, quod inimici eius
3 dissidentis suos sensus aperturi forent.   tali consilio probato excepit has partes ipse Callicrates et se armat imprudentia Dionis.   ad eum interficiundum socios conquirit, adversarios eius convenit, coniuratione
4 confirmat.   res, multis consciis quae gereretur, elata defertur ad Aristomachen, sororem Dionis, uxoremque Areten. illae timore perterritae convenient, cuius de periculo timebant.   at ille negat a Callicrate fieri sibi insidias, sed illa, quae agerentur, fieri praecepto suo.   mulieres nihilo setius Callicratem in
5 aedem Proserpinae deducunt ac iurare cogunt, nihil ab illo periculi fore Dioni.   ille hac religione non

modo non est deterritus, sed ad maturandum con-
citatus est, verens ne prius consilium aperiretur uums,
quam conata perfecisset.

IX

CH. 9.   *Dion was murdered in his own home by agents of*
Callicrates (353).

Hac mente proximo die festo, cum a conventu se
remotum Dion domi teneret atque in conclavi edito
recubuisset, consciis facinoris loca munitiora oppidi
tradit, domum custodiis saepit, a foribus qui non
discedant, certos praeficit, navem triremem armatis
ornat Philostratoque, fratri suo, tradit eamque in 2
portu agitari iubet, ut si exercere remiges vellet,
cogitans, si forte consiliis obstitisset fortuna, ut haberet, qua fugeret ad salutem. suorum autem e 3
numero Zacynthios adulescentes quosdam eligit cum
audacissimos tum viribus maximis, hisque dat negotium, ad Dionem eant inermes, sic ut conveniendi
eius gratia viderentur venire. hi propter notitiam 4
sunt intromissi. at illi ut limen eius intrarant,
foribus obseratis in lecto cubantem invadunt, colli-
gant: fit strepitus, adeo ut exaudiri possit foris. hic, 5
sicut ante saepe dictum est, quam invisa sit singularis
potentia et miseranda vita, qui se metui quam amari
malunt, cuivis facile intellectu fuit. namque illi ipsi 6
custodes, si propria fuissent voluntate, foribus effractis
servare eum potuissent, quod illi inermes telum foris
flagitantes vivum tenebant. cui cum succurreret
nemo, Lyco quidam Syracusanus per fenestras glad-
ium dedit, quo Dion interfectus est.

X

Ch. 10. *After his death he was widely lamented; and remembered only as the liberator of his country.*

Confecta caede, cum multitudo visendi gratia introisset, nonnulli ab insciis pro noxiis conciduntur. nam celeri rumore dilato, Dioni vim allatam, multi concurrerant, quibus tale facinus displicebat. hi falsa suspicione ducti immerentes ut sceleratos occi-
2 dunt. huius de morte ut palam factum est, mirabiliter vulgi mutata est voluntas. nam qui vivum eum tyrannum vocitarant, eidem liberatorem patriae tyrannique expulsorem praedicabant. sic subito misericordia odio successerat, ut eum suo sanguine ab
3 Acherunte, si possent, cuperent redimere. itaque in urbe celeberrimo loco, elatus publice, sepulcri monumento donatus est. diem obiit circiter annos LV natus, quartum post annum, quam ex Peloponneso in Siciliam redierat.

ATTICUS

109–32 B.C.

The biography of Atticus, the last and much the longest of the twenty-five 'Lives,' was presumably the climax of the whole work. Nepos is now for the first time writing from personal knowledge, and the abundance of his material leads him to change his tactics. The obvious, chronological method which he used successfully for his other biographies is at first followed half-heartedly, and then abandoned. The effect is unfortunate. We wander along through a list of Atticus' habits and virtues until suddenly, in Chap. XIX, the postscript commands our attention and brings the work to a satisfactory end.

This defect of style, however, does not lessen the interest of Nepos' subject matter. Atticus' chief claim to fame is that he was the friend of Cicero and the publisher of his works, especially his voluminous and highly informative Correspondence. Over 400 letters from Cicero to Atticus himself have been preserved. While they throw light indirectly upon their recipient, they make us curious to know more about the man whose advice and encouragement Cicero sought regularly for twenty-four years. We wonder too by what cunning he survived the succession of shambles in which hundreds of thousands of other Romans lost their lives.

When we remember that Nepos was writing of a friend and a man of some consequence in the world, we shall not be surprised to find that Atticus could do no wrong, or that his survival was due not to cunning but to his lifelong principles of neutrality in politics and kindness to those in distress. What is really surprising is that this explanation appears to be substantially correct. In his eulogies Nepos may occasionally overstep the mark, and there are some silences—about Atticus' wife, for example—which may be significant. But otherwise there seems no reason to reject his account of a cultured and kindly Epicurean, who in a dark period of Rome's history was respected by friend and foe alike.

I

CH. 1. *Atticus was born of a wealthy and cultured family. At school he was an able pupil among some distinguished contemporaries.*

T. Pomponius Atticus, ab origine ultima stirpis Romanae generatus, perpetuo a maioribus acceptam
2 equestrem obtinuit dignitatem. patre usus est diligente et, ut tum erant tempora, diti inprimisque studioso litterarum. hic, prout ipse amabat litteras, omnibus doctrinis, quibus puerilis aetas impertiri
3 debet, filium erudivit. erat autem in puero praeter docilitatem ingenii summa suavitas oris atque vocis, ut non solum celeriter acciperet quae tradebantur, sed etiam excellenter pronuntiaret. qua ex re in pueritia nobilis inter aequales ferebatur clariusque exsplendescebat, quam generosi condiscipuli animo aequo ferre
4 possent. itaque incitabat omnes studio suo, quo in numero fuerunt L. Torquatus, C. Marius filius, M. Cicero: quos consuetudine sua sic devinxit, ut nemo his perpetuo fuerit carior.

II

CH. 2. *Having lost his father he migrated to Athens (c. 87) to avoid the violence of Roman politics. His financial help won him the gratitude of the Athenians.*

Pater mature decessit. ipse adulescentulus propter affinitatem P. Sulpicii, qui tribunus pl. interfectus est, non expers fuit illius periculi: namque Anicia, Pomponii consobrina, nupserat Servio, fratri Sulpicii.
2 itaque interfecto Sulpicio posteaquam vidit Cinnano tumultu civitatem esse perturbatam neque sibi dari

facultatem pro dignitate vivendi, quin alterutram
partem offenderet, dissociatis animis civium, cum alii
Sullanis, alii Cinnanis faverent partibus, idoneum
tempus ratus studiis obsequendi suis Athenas se contulit.   neque eo setius adulescentem Marium hostem
iudicatum iuvit opibus suis, cuius fugam pecunia
sublevavit. ac ne illa peregrinatio detrimentum 3
aliquod afferret rei familiari, eodem magnam partem
fortunarum traiecit suarum.   hic ita vixit, ut universis
Atheniensibus merito esset carissimus.   nam praeter 4
gratiam, quae iam in adulescentulo magna erat, saepe
suis opibus inopiam eorum publicam levavit.   cum
enim versuram facere publice necesse esset neque eius
condicionem aequam haberent, semper se interposuit,
atque ita ut neque usuram umquam ab iis acceperit
neque longius, quam dictum esset, debere passus sit.
quod utrumque erat iis salutare: nam neque indul- 5
gendo inveterascere eorum aes alienum patiebatur
neque multiplicandis usuris crescere. auxit hoc
officium alia quoque liberalitate: nam universos
frumento donavit, ita ut singulis VI modii tritici
darentur, qui modus mensurae medimnus Athenis
appellatur.

III

CH. 3.   *So high was their regard for him that later they
erected statues both to Atticus and to his agent.*

Hic autem sic se gerebat, ut communis infimis, par
principibus videretur.   quo factum est ut huic omnes
honores, quos possent, publice haberent civemque
facere studerent: quo beneficio ille uti noluit [quod
nonnulli ita interpretantur, amitti civitatem Roman-
am alia ascita]. quamdiu adfuit, ne qua sibi statua

poneretur, restitit, absens prohibere non potuit.
2 itaque aliquot ipsi et Phidiae locis sanctissimis posuer-
unt: hunc enim in omni procuratione rei publicae
3 actorem auctoremque habebant. igitur primum
illud munus fortunae, quod in ea potissimum urbe
natus est, in qua domicilium orbis terrarum esset
imperii, ut eandem et patriam haberet et domum;
hoc specimen prudentiae, quod, cum in eam se civitatem contulisset, quae antiquitate, humanitate doc-
trinaque praestaret omnes, unus ei fuit carissimus.

IV

Cн. 4. *Sulla on his way back from Asia was delighted by*
the young man's linguistic ability.   Atticus tactfully declined
an invitation to return with him, and except for occasional visits
to Rome to help his friends remained at Athens until 65 B.C.

Huc ex Asia Sulla decedens cum venisset, quamdiu
ibi fuit, secum habuit Pomponium, captus adulescentis et humanitate et doctrina. sic enim Graece
loquebatur, ut Athenis natus videretur; tanta autem
suavitas erat sermonis Latini, ut appareret in eo
nativum quendam leporem esse, non ascitum. idem
poemata pronuntiabat et Graece et Latine sic, ut
2 supra nihil posset addi. quibus rebus factum est ut
Sulla nusquam ab se dimitteret cuperetque secum
deducere.   qui cum persuadere tentaret, 'noli, oro te,'
inquit Pomponius 'adversum eos me velle ducere, cum
quibus ne contra te arma ferrem, Italiam reliqui.'   at
Sulla adulescentis officio collaudato omnia munera ei,
quae Athenis acceperat, proficiscens iussit deferri.
3 Hic complures annos moratus, cum et rei familiari
tantum operae daret, quantum non indiligens deberet

pater familias, et omnia reliqua tempora aut litteris
aut Atheniensium rei publicae tribueret, nihilo minus
amicis urbana officia praestitit. nam et ad comitia 4
eorum ventitavit et, si qua res maior acta est, non
defuit. sicut Ciceroni in omnibus eius periculis
singularem fidem praebuit: cui ex patria fugienti HS
ducenta et quinquaginta milia donavit. tranquillatis 5
autem rebus Romanis remigravit Romam, ut opinor
L. Cotta et L. Torquato consulibus: quem disceden-
tem sic universa civitas Atheniensium prosecuta est, ut
lacrimis desiderii futuri dolorem indicaret.

V

Сн. 5.   *His success in humouring a difficult uncle brought
him a handsome legacy.   He maintained a close friendship
with the rival orators Cicero and Hortensius.*

Habebat avunculum Q. Caecilium, equitem Ro-
manum, familiarem L. Luculli, divitem, difficillima
natura: cuius sic asperitatem veritus est, ut, quem
nemo ferre posset, huius sine offensione ad summam
senectutem retinuerit benevolentiam. quo facto 2
tulit pietatis fructum.   Caecilius enim moriens testamento adoptavit eum heredemque fecit ex dodrante:
ex qua hereditate accepit circiter centies sestertium.
erat nupta soror Attici Q. Tullio Ciceroni, easque 3
nuptias M. Cicero conciliarat, cum quo a condisci-
pulatu vivebat coniunctissime, multo etiam familiarius quam cum Quinto, ut iudicari possit plus in
amicitia valere similitudinem morum quam affinitatem. utebatur autem intime Q. Hortensio, qui, iis 4
temporibus principatum eloquentiae tenebat, ut
intellegi non posset, uter eum plus diligeret, Cicero an

Hortensius: et, id quod erat difficillimum, efficiebat
ut, inter quos tantae laudis esset aemulatio, nulla
intercederet obtrectatio essetque talium virorum
copula.

VI

CH. 6.   *Atticus' political sympathies were with the Senate
but he deliberately took no part in public life.*

In re publica ita est versatus, ut semper optimarum
partium et esset et existimaretur, neque tamen se
civilibus fluctibus committeret, quod non magis eos in
sua potestate existimabat esse, qui se his dedissent,
2 quam qui maritimis iactarentur. honores non petiit,
cum ei paterent propter vel gratiam vel dignitatem:
quod neque peti more maiorum neque capi possent
conservatis legibus in tam effusi ambitus largitionibus
neque geri e re publica sine periculo corruptis civitatis
3 moribus, ad hastam publicam numquam accessit.
nullius rei neque praes neque manceps factus est.
neminem neque suo nomine neque subscribens accus-
avit, in ius de sua re numquam iit, iudicium nullum
4 habuit. multorum consulum praetorumque prae-
fecturas delatas sic accepit, ut neminem in provinciam
sit secutus, honore fuerit contentus, rei familiaris
despexerit fructum: qui ne cum Q. quidem Cicerone
voluerit ire in Asiam, cum apud eum legati locum
obtinere posset. non enim decere se arbitrabatur,
cum praeturam gerere noluisset, asseclam esse prae-
5 toris. qua in re non solum dignitati serviebat, sed
etiam tranquillitati, cum suspiciones quoque vitaret
criminum. quo fiebat ut eius observantia omnibus
esset carior, cum eam officio, non timori neque spei
tribui viderent.

VII

CH. 7. During the Civil War Caesar was pleased that Atticus remained in Rome. He gave generous help, however, to any friends who wished to fight for Pompey.

Incidit Caesarianum civile bellum, cum haberet annos circiter sexaginta. usus est aetatis vacatione neque se quoquam movit ex urbe. quae amicis suis opus fuerant ad Pompeium proficiscentibus, omnia ex sua re familiari dedit, ipsum Pompeium coniunctum non offendit. nullum ab eo habebat ornamentum, ut 2 ceteri, qui per eum aut honores aut divitias ceperant: quorum partim invitissimi castra sunt secuti, partim summa cum eius offensione domi remanserunt. Attici autem quies tantopere Caesari fuit grata, ut 3 victor, cum privatis pecunias per epistulas imperaret, huic non solum molestus non fuerit, sed etiam sororis filium et Q. Ciceronem ex Pompei castris concesserit. sic vetere instituto vitae effugit nova pericula.

VIII

CH. 8. After Caesar's murder Atticus declined to sponsor a fund for the 'Liberators'; later when their cause seemed desperate he sent Brutus two generous donations.

Secutum est illud tempus occiso Caesare quo res publica penes Brutos videretur esse et Cassium ac tota civitas se ad eos convertisse videretur. sic M. Bruto 2 usus est, ut nullo ille adulescens aequali familiarius quam hoc sene, neque solum eum principem consilii haberet, sed etiam in convictu. excogitatum 3 est a quibusdam, ut privatum aerarium Caesaris

D

interfectoribus ab equitibus Romanis constitueretur.
id facile effici posse arbitrati sunt, si principes eius
ordinis pecunias contulissent. itaque appellatus est a
C. Flavio, Bruti familiari, Atticus, ut eius rei princeps
4 esse vellet. at ille, qui officia amicis praestanda sine
factione existimaret semperque a talibus se consiliis
removisset, respondit: si quid Brutus de suis facultati-
bus uti voluisset, usurum, quantum eae paterentur,
sed neque cum quoquam de ea re collocuturum neque
coiturum. sic ille consensionis globus huius unius
5 dissensione disiectus est. neque multo post superior
esse coepit Antonius, ita ut Brutus et Cassius destituta
tutela provinciarum, quae iis dicis causa datae erant
a consule, desperatis rebus in exsilium proficisceren-
6 tur. Atticus, qui pecuniam simul cum ceteris conferre noluerat florenti illi parti, abiecto Bruto Italia-
que cedenti HS centum milia muneri misit. eidem
in Epiro absens trecenta iussit dari, neque eo magis
potenti adulatus est Antonio neque desperatos reliquit.

IX

CH. 9. *Atticus was criticised for coming to the rescue of
Antony's wife and friends after his defeat at Mutina.*

Secutum est bellum gestum apud Mutinam. in
quo si tantum eum prudentem dicam, minus quam
debeam praedicem, cum ille potius divinus fuerit, si
divinatio appellanda est perpetua naturalis bonitas,
quae nullis casibus agitur neque minuitur. hostis
2 Antoniu siudicatus Italia cesserat: spes restituendi
nulla erat. non solum inimici, qui tum erant poten-
tissimi et plurimi, sed etiam qui adversariis eius se
dabant et in eo laedendo aliquam consecuturos

sperabant commoditatem, Antonii familiares inseque-
bantur, uxorem Fulviam omnibus rebus spoliare
cupiebant, liberos etiam exstinguere parabant. Atti- 3
cus, cum Ciceronis intima familiaritate uteretur,
amicissimus esset Bruto, non modo nihil iis indulsit ad
Antonium violandum, sed e contrario familiares eius
ex urbe profugientes, quantum potuit, texit, quibus
rebus indiguerunt, adiuvit. P. vero Volumnio ea 4
tribuit, ut plura a parente proficisci non potuerint.
ipsi autem Fulviae, cum litibus distineretur magnisque
terroribus vexaretur, tanta diligentia officium suum
praestitit, ut nullum illa stiterit vadimonium sine
Attico, sponsor omnium rerum fuerit. quin etiam, 5
cum illa fundum secunda fortuna emisset in diem
neque post calamitatem versuram facere potuisset,
ille se interposuit pecuniamque sine faenore sineque
ulla stipulatione credidit, maximum existimans quaestum, memorem gratumque cognosci, simulque
aperire se non fortunae, sed hominibus solere esse
amicum. quae cum faciebat, nemo eum temporis 6
causa facere poterat existimare: nemini enim in
opinionem veniebat Antonium rerum potiturum.
sed sensim is a nonnullis optimatibus reprehende- 7
batur, quod parum odisse malos cives videretur. ille
autem, sui iudicii, potius quid se facere par esset
intuebatur quam quid alii laudaturi forent.

X

CH. 10. *But when Antony returned as a Triumvir his
gratitude saved not merely Atticus himself from proscription.*

Conversa subito fortuna est. ut Antonius rediit in
Italiam, nemo non magno in periculo Atticum

putarat propter intimam familiaritatem Ciceronis et
2 Bruti. itaque ad adventum imperatorum de foro
decesserat, timens proscriptionem, latebatque apud
P. Volumnium, cui, ut ostendimus, paulo ante opem
tulerat (tanta varietas iis temporibus fuit fortunae, ut
modo hi, modo illi in summo essent aut fastigio aut
periculo), habebatque secum Q. Gellium Canum,
aequalem simillimumque sui. hoc quoque sit Attici
bonitatis exemplum, quod cum eo, quem puerum in
ludo cognorat, adeo coniuncte vixit, ut ad extremam
4 aetatem amicitia eorum creverit. Antonius autem,
etsi tanto odio ferebatur in Ciceronem, ut non solum
ei, sed etiam omnibus eius amicis esset inimicus eosque
vellet proscribere multis hortantibus, tamen Attici
memor fuit officii et ei, cum requisisset, ubinam esset,
sua manu scripsit, ne timeret statimque ad se veniret:
se eum et illius causa Canum de proscriptorum
5 numero exemisse. ac ne quod periculum incideret,
quod noctu fiebat, praesidium ei misit. sic Atticus in
summo timore non solum sibi, sed etiam ei, quem
carissimum habebat, praesidio fuit neque enim suae
solum a quoquam auxilium petiit salutis, [sed con-
iuncti,] ut appareret nullam seiunctam sibi ab eo
6 velle fortunam. quodsi gubernator praecipua laude
fertur, qui navem ex hieme marique scopuloso servat,
cur non singularis eius existimetur prudentia, qui ex
tot tamque gravibus procellis civilibus ad incolumi-
tatem pervenit?

XI

CH. 11. *During the proscriptions and after Philippi he did all he could to help those in danger, with no ulterior motive.*

Quibus ex malis ut se emersit, nihil aliud egit quam

ut *quam* plurimis, quibus rebus posset, esset auxilio.
cum proscriptos praemiis imperatorum vulgus con-
quireret, nemo in Epirum venit, cui res ulla defuerit:
nemini non ibi perpetuo manendi potestas facta est;
quin etiam post proelium Philippense interitumque 2
C. Cassi et M. Bruti L. Iulium Mocillam praetorium
et filium eius Aulumque Torquatum ceterosque pari
fortuna perculsos instituit tueri atque ex Epiro iis
omnia Samothraciam supportari iussit. difficile est
omnia persequi et non necessarium. illud unum 3
intellegi volumus, illius liberalitatem neque temporariam neque callidam fuisse. id ex ipsis rebus ac 4
temporibus iudicari potest, quod non florentibus se
venditavit, sed afflictis semper succurrit: qui quidem
Serviliam, Bruti matrem, non minus post mortem
eius quam florentem coluerit. sic liberalitate utens 5
nullas inimicitias gessit, quod neque laedebat quemquam neque, si quam iniuriam acceperat, non malebat oblivisci quam ulcisci. idem immortali memoria
percepta retinebat beneficia; quae autem ipse tri-
buerat, tam diu meminerat, quoad ille gratus erat, qui
acceperat. itaque hic fecit ut vere dictum videatur:

Sui cuíque mores fíngunt fortunam hóminibus. 6
neque tamen ille prius fortunam quam se ipse finxit,
qui cavit ne qua in re iure plecteretur.

XII

CH. 12. *He was greatly honoured by his daughter's*
marriage to Agrippa, the close friend of Octavian. The
marriage was arranged by Antony, whose assistance Atticus
sought only in order to serve his friends.

His igitur rebus effecit ut M. Vipsanius Agrippa,

intima familiaritate coniunctus adulescenti Caesari,
cum propter suam gratiam et Caesaris potentiam
nullius condicionis non haberet potestatem, potissimum eius deligeret affinitatem praeoptaretque equitis
2 Romani filiam generosarum nuptiis. atque harum
nuptiarum conciliator fuit (non est enim celandum)
M. Antonius, triumvir rei publicae, cuius gratia cum
augere possessiones posset suas, tantum afuit a cupiditate pecuniae, ut nulla in re usus sit ea nisi in depre-
3 candis amicorum aut periculis aut incommodis. quod
quidem sub ipsa proscriptione perillustre fuit. nam
cum L. Saufei equitis Romani, aequalis sui, qui
complures annos studio ductus philosophiae Athenis
habitabat habebatque in Italia pretiosas possessiones,
triumviri bona vendidissent consuetudine ea, qua tum
res gerebantur, Attici labore atque industria factum
est ut eodem nuntio Saufeius fieret certior se patri-
4 monium amisisse et recuperasse. idem L. Iulium
Calidum, quem post Lucreti Catullique mortem
multo elegantissimum poetam nostram tulisse aetatem
vere videor posse contendere, neque minus virum
bonum optimisque artibus eruditum; quem post
proscriptionem equitum propter magnas eius Afri-
canas possessiones in proscriptorum numerum a P.
Volumnio, praefecto fabrum Antonii, absentem
5 relatum expedivit. quod in praesenti utrum ei
laboriosius an gloriosius fuerit, difficile est iudicare,
quod in eorum periculis non secus absentes quam
praesentes maicos Attico esse curae cognitum est.

XIII

CH. 13.   *He lived elegantly but without ostentation.*

Neque vero ille vir minus bonus pater familias

habitus est quam civis. nam cum esset pecuniosus,
nemo illo minus fuit emax, minus aedificator. neque
tamen non in primis bene habitavit omnibusque
optimis rebus usus est. nam domum habuit in colle 2
Quirinali Tamphilianam, ab avunculo hereditate
relictam, cuius amoenitas non aedificio, sed silva
constabat: ipsum enim tectum antiquitus constitutum
plus salis quam sumptus habebat: in quo nihil commutavit, nisi si quid vetustate coactus est. usus est 3
familia, si utilitate iudicandum est, optima, si forma,
vix mediocri. namque in ea erant pueri litteratissimi,
anagnostae optimi et plurimi librarii, ut ne pedisequus quidem quisquam esset, qui non utrumque
horum pulchre facere posset, pari modo artifices
ceteri, quos cultus domesticus desiderat, apprime
boni. neque tamen horum quemquam nisi domi 4
natum domique factum habuit: quod est signum non
solum continentiae, sed etiam diligentiae. nam et
non intemperanter concupiscere, quod a plurimis
videas, continentis debet duci, et potius diligentia
quam pretio parare non mediocris est industriae.
elegans, non magnificus, splendidus, non sumptuosus: 5
omnisque diligentia munditiam, non affluentiam
affectabat. supellex modica, non multa, ut in neutram partem conspici posset. nec praeteribo, quam- 6
quam nonnullis leve visum iri putem, cum in primis
lautus esset eques Romanus et non parum liberaliter
domum suam omnium ordinum homines invitaret,
scimus non amplius quam terna milia peraeque in
singulos menses ex ephemeride eum expensum
sumptui ferre solitum. atque hoc non auditum, sed 7
cognitum praedicamus: saepe enim propter familiaritatem domesticis rebus interfuimus.

XIV

CH. 14. *The entertainment at his dinner parties was in the best of taste. The legacy from his uncle did not change his way of life.*

Nemo in convivio eius aliud acroama audivit quam anagnosten, quod nos quidem iucundissimum arbitramur; neque umquam sine aliqua lectione apud eum cenatum est, ut non minus animo quam ventre
2 convivae delectarentur: namque eos vocabat, quorum mores a suis non abhorrerent. cum tanta pecuniae facta esset accessio, nihil de cotidiano cultu mutavit, nihil de vitae consuetudine, tantaque usus est moderatione, ut neque in sestertio viciens, quod a patre acceperat, parum se splendide gesserit neque in sestertio centies affluentius vixerit, quam instituerat,
3 parique fastigio steterit in utraque fortuna. nullos habuit hortos, nullam suburbanam aut maritiman sumptuosam villam, neque in Italia, praeter Arretinum et Nomentanum, rusticum praedium, omnisque eius pecuniae reditus constabat in Epiroticis et urbanis possessionibus. ex quo cognosci potest usum eum pecuniae non magnitudine, sed ratione metiri solitum.

XV

CH. 15. *Scrupulously honest, he made it a point of honour to keep his promises.*

Mendacium neque dicebat neque pati poterat. itaque eius comitas non sine severitate erat neque

gravitas sine facilitate, ut difficile esset intellectu,
utrum eum amici magis vererentur an amarent.
quidquid rogabatur, religiose promittebat, quod non
liberalis, sed levis arbitrabatur polliceri quod praestare non posset. idem in nitendo, quod semel 2
annuisset, tanta erat cura, ut non mandatam, sed
suam rem videretur agere. numquam suscepti
negotii eum pertaesum est: suam enim existima-
tionem in ea re agi putabat, qua nihil habebat carius.
quo fiebat ut omnia Ciceronum, Catonis Marci, Q. 3
Hortensi, Auli Torquati, multorum praeterea equitum
Romanorum negotia procuraret. ex quo iudicari
poterat non inertia, sed iudicio fugisse rei publicae
procurationem.

XVI

CH. 16. *He maintained successful friendships with both
old and young. Cicero was especially attached to him, as
his letters show.*

Humanitatis vero nullum adferre maius testimon-
ium possum, quam quod adulescens idem seni Sullae
fuit iucundissimus, senex adulescenti M. Bruto,
cum aequalibus autem suis Q. Hortensio et M.
Cicerone sic vixit, ut iudicare difficile sit, cui aetati
fuerit aptissimus. quamquam eum praecipue dilexit
Cicero, ut ne frater quidem ei Quintus carior fuerit
aut familiarior. ei rei sunt indicio praeter eos libros, 3
in quibus de eo facit mentionem, qui in vulgus sunt
editi, XVI volumina epistularum, ab consulatu eius
usque ad extremum tempus ad Atticum missarum:
quae qui legat, non multum desideret historiam con-
textam eorum temporum. sic enim omnia de studiis 4

principum, vitiis ducum, mutationibus rei publicae
perscripta sunt, ut nihil in eis non appareat et facile
existimari possit, prudentiam quodam modo esse
divinationem.   non enim Cicero ea solum, quae vivo
se acciderunt, futura praedixit, sed etiam, quae nunc
usu veniunt, cecinit ut vates.

XVII

CH. 17.   *He never quarrelled with his mother or sister.*

De pietate autem Attici quid plura commemorem?
cum hoc ipsum vere gloriantem audierim in funere
matris suae, quam extulit annorum nonaginta, cum
esset septem et sexaginta, se numquam cum matre in
gratiam redisse, numquam cum sorore fuisse in
2 simultate, quam prope aequalem habebat.   quod est
signum aut nullam umquam inter eos querimoniam
intercessisse, aut hunc ea fuisse in suos indulgentia, ut,
3 quos amare deberet, irasci eis nefas duceret.   neque
id fecit natura solum, quamquam omnes ei paremus,
sed etiam doctrina: nam principum philosophorum
ita percepta habuit praecepta, ut iis ad vitam agen-
dam, non ad ostentationem uteretur.

XVIII

CH. 18.   *His historical researches led to various forms of*
literary activity in both prose and verse.

Moris etiam maiorum summus imitator fuit anti-
quitatisque amator, quam adeo diligenter habuit
cognitam, ut eam totam in eo volumine exposuerit,
2 quo magistratus ordinavit.   nulla enim lex neque pax

neque bellum neque res illustris est populi Romani,
quae non in eo suo tempore sit notata, et, quod difficillimum fuit, sic familiarum originem subtexuit, ut
ex eo clarorum virorum propagines possimus cog-
noscere.   fecit hoc idem separatim in aliis libris, ut 3
M. Bruti rogatu Iuniam familiam a stirpe ad hanc
aetatem ordine enumeraverit, notans, quis a quo ortus
quos honores quibusque temporibus cepisset: pari 4
modo Marcelli Claudi de Marcellorum, Scipionis
Corneli et Fabi Maximi Fabiorum et Aemiliorum.
quibus libris nihil potest esse dulcius iis, qui aliquam
cupiditatem habent notitiae clarorum virorum.
attigit poeticen quoque, credimus, ne eius expers esset 5
suavitatis.   namque versibus, qui honore rerumque
gestarum amplitudine ceteros populi Romani praestiterunt, exposuit ita, ut sub singulorum imaginibus 6
facta magistratusque eorum non amplius quaternis
quinisve versibus descripserit: quod vix credendum
sit tantas res tam breviter potuisse declarari. est etiam
unus liber Graece confectus, de consuatlu Ciceronis.

XIX

CH. 19. *A postscript: The betrothal of his infant granddaughter to the emperor's stepson (probably* 34 B.C.) *gave
Atticus frequent access to Octavian himself.*

Hactenus Attico vivo edita a nobis sunt. nunc,
quoniam fortuna nos superstites ei esse voluit, reliqua
persequemur et, quantum potuerimus, rerum exem-
plis lectores docebimus, sicut supra significavimus,
suos cuique mores plerumque conciliare fortunam.
namque hic contentus ordine equestri, quo erat ortus, 2
in adfinitatem pervenit imperatoris divi fili, cum iam

ante familiaritatem eius esset consecutus nulla alia re
quam elegantia vitae, qua ceteros ceperat principes,
3 civitatis dignitate pari, fortuna humiliores. tanta
enim prosperitas Caesarem est consecuta, ut nihil ei
non tribuerit fortuna, quod cuiquam ante detulerit, et
conciliarit, quod nemo adhuc civis Romanus quivit
4 consequi. nata est autem Attico neptis ex Agrippa,
cui virginem filiam collocarat. hanc Caesar vix
anniculam Ti. Claudio Neroni, Drusilla nato, priv-
igno suo, despondit: quae coniunctio necessitudinem
eorum sanxit, familiaritatem reddidit frequentiorem.

XX

CH. 20. *Whether in Rome or abroad Octavian would
write to him almost daily. Antony too was a constant
correspondent. To retain the friendship of both required
great tact.*

Quamvis ante haec sponsalia non solum, cum ab
urbe abesset, numquam ad suorum quemquam
litteras misit, quin Attico mitteret, quid ageret, in
primis quid legeret quibusque in locis et quamdiu
2 esset moraturus, sed etiam, cum esset in urbe et
propter infinitas suas occupationes minus saepe, quam
vellet, Attico frueretur, nullus dies temere intercessit,
quo non ad eum scriberet, cum modo aliquid de
antiquitate ab eo requireret, modo aliquam quaes-
tionem poeticam ei proponeret, interdum iocans eius
3 verbosiores eliceret epistulas. ex quo accidit, cum
aedis Iovis Feretri in Capitolio, ab Romulo constituta,
vetustate atque incuria detecta prolaberetur, ut Attici
4 admonitu Caesar eam reficiendam curaret. neque
vero a M. Antonio minus absens litteris colebatur,

adeo ut accurate ille ex ultumis terris, quid ageret,
curae sibi haberet certiorem facere Atticum. hoc 5
quale sit, facilius existimabit is, qui iudicare poterit,
quantae sit sapientiae eorum retinere usum beni-
volentiamque, inter quos maximarum rerum non
solum aemulatio, sed obtrectatio tanta intercedebat,
quantam fuit incidere necesse inter Caesarem atque
Antonium, cum se uterque principem non solum urbis
Romae, sed orbis terrarum esse cuperet.

XXI

CH. 21. *At the age of seventy-seven he contracted an
incurable illness. Summoning his friends he announced his
decision to end his life.*

Tali modo cum VII et LXX annos complesset atque
ad extremam senectutem non minus dignitate quam
gratia fortunaque crevisset (multas enim hereditates
nulla alia re quam bonitate consecutus tantaque
prosperitate usus est valetudinis, ut annis triginta
medicina non indiguisset) nactus est morbum, quem 2
initio et ipse et medici contempserunt: nam putarunt
esse tenesmon, cui remedia celeria faciliaque pro-
ponebantur. in hoc cum tres menses sine ullis dolori- 3
bus, praeterquam quos ex curatione capiebat, con-
sumpsisset, subito tanta vis morbi in imum intestinum
prorupit, ut extremo tempore per lumbos fistulae
puris eruperint. atque hoc priusquam ei accideret, 4
postquam in dies dolores accrescere febresque acces-
sisse sensit, Agrippam generum ad se accersi iussit et
cum eo L. Cornelium Balbum Sextumque Peducaeum.
hos ut venisse vidit, in cubitum innixus 'quantam' 5
inquit 'curam diligentiamque in valetudine mea

tuenda hoc tempore adhibuerim, cum vos testes
habeam, nihil necesse est pluribus verbis commemo-
rare. quibus quoniam, ut spero, satisfeci, me nihil
reliqui fecisse, quod ad sanandum me pertineret,
reliquum est ut egomet mihi consulam. id vos
6 ignorare nolui: nam mihi stat alere morbum desinere.
namque his diebus quidquid cibi sumpsi, ita produxi
vitam, ut auxerim dolores sine spe salutis. quare a
vobis peto, primum ut consilium probetis meum,
deinde ne frustra dehortando impedire conemini.'

XXII

Cн. 22. *In spite of protests he starved himself to death,*
31*st March* 32 B.C.

Hac oratione habita tanta constantia vocis atque
vultus, ut non ex vita, sed ex domo in domum videre-
2 tur migrare, cum quidem Agrippa eum flens atque
osculans oraret atque obsecraret, ne id quod natura
cogeret ipse quoque sibi acceleraret, et quoniam tum
quoque posset temporibus superesse, se sibi suisque
reservaret, precis eius taciturna sua obstinatione
3 depressit. sic cum biduum cibo se abstinuisset,
subito febris decessit leviorque morbus esse coepit.
tamen propositum nihilo setius peregit itaque die
quinto, postquam id consilium inierat, pridie kal.
Aprilis Cn. Domitio C. Sosio consulibus decessit.
4 elatus est in lecticula, ut ipse praescripserat, sine ulla
pompa funeris, comitantibus omnibus bonis, maxima
vulgi frequentia. sepultus est iuxta viam Appiam
ad quintum lapidem in monumento Q. Caecili,
avunculi sui.

NOTES

I

1. **Alcibiades . . . Atheniensis.** Nepos begins each of his *Lives of Famous Foreign Generals* in this way, giving name, parentage when known, and nationality.

in hoc . . . videtur experta. The subject of both the main clause and the Indirect Question is *natura*. 'In his case Nature seems to have tried what she could achieve.'

memoriae prodiderunt: 'have handed down to the memory', sc. of posterity, i.e. all the historians who have written about him.

2. **amplissima.** This word is used as a term of approval in a wide variety of contexts. Here it means 'leading', 'flourishing'. At the time when Alcibiades was born, *c.* 450 B.C., the alliance of maritime states which had been formed under Athenian leadership to forestall any further Persian attempt to invade Greece had developed into an Athenian empire. Supported by annual contributions of ships or money from her subject allies, Athens could fairly claim to be the most powerful single state in Greece.

summo genera: ablative of origin with *natus*, 'born of a very distinguished family'.

ut . . . valeret. Result clause, lit. 'so that he had power among the foremost by his speaking', i.e. he was a very effective speaker.

3. **vita quam victu:** *vita* here is his public life, *victus* his style of living, e.g. his clothing, food and drink, his racing stable which was famous throughout Greece. In 420 (or possibly 416) he entered no less than seven chariots for the Olympic games, more than anyone had ever entered before. With three of them he carried off 1st, 2nd and either 3rd of 4th prizes, a tremendous triumph both for himself and Athens.

4. **temporibus . . . serviens:** i.e. adjusting his conduct to prevailing circumstances.

57

II

1. **in domo Pericli.** When domus means 'house' merely in the sense of 'building' it has prepositions like an ordinary noun. Cf. *in domo sua*, III. 6 inf.

For Pericles and Socrates see Index of Proper Names.

privignus . . . fuisse dicitur. This statement is scarcely credible, for there is no evidence that Dinarche his mother ever married Pericles and good reason to believe she did not. She did, however, come under his guardianship in 447 along with her two baby sons, when Clinias was killed in the Battle of Coronea. Like Pericles' mother, Dinarche belonged to the great Alcmaeonid family and Athenian law required a widow to pass under the control of her nearest male relative. Diodorus, a Greek historian writing slightly later that Nepos, says Alcibiades was Pericles' nephew.

ut, si ipse . . .: 'so that if he (Alc.) himself were wanting to arrange (his own life), he could neither imagine more advantages, nor attain greater ones than . . .'

III

1. **Bello Peloponnesio.** See Introduction pp. 5–6.

auctoritate: 'instigation'.

bellum Syracusanis indixerunt. In an attempt to break the stalemate of the first ten years of the Peloponnesian War Alcibiades urged the Athenians to conquer Sicily and secure what they believed to be the fabulous wealth of the island. Carried away by his eloquence they staked their remaining resources on two huge expeditions. Deprived of Alcibiades' inspiring leadership, however (cf. IV. 3 inf.), these failed completely in their main objective, of capturing Syracuse, the chief city of Sicily. From the final disaster in 413 B.C. scarcely a single Athenian soldier survived.

ad quod gerendum: a common idiom for expressing purpose, 'to wage this war'. Cf. *ad patriam liberandam*, IX. 4 inf.

2. **prius quam classis exiret.** The prospective subjunctive is used because at the time of this incident the

departure of their fleet was something to which the Athenians were still looking forward. As it did in fact sail, an indicative could equally well have been used.

Hermae: Heads of the god Hermes, mounted on square pillars, were a common sight in the streets and public places of Athens. He was originally worshipped as a giver of fertility. Hence the superstitious horror at the possible consequences of the sacrilege.

Mercurius: the Roman counterpart of the Greek Hermes, both being messengers of the gods. The transition, however, is awkward.

3. **multitudini.** The dative follows the compound verb. After such verbs two constructions are theoretically possible: either the compounding preposition is repeated, with the appropriate case (*in multitudinem*), or a plain dative is used (*multitudini*). In practice the latter is very much commoner.

pertineret: subjunctive because it is the verb of a subordinate clause in indirect speech, following *appareret*.

repentina vis: 'a sudden (act of) violence', 'a coup d'état'.

quae . . . opprimeret. This relative clause may be regarded as expressing either purpose or result.

4. **hoc maxime convenire . . . videbatur:** 'suspicion seemed to point especially to Alcibiades'. Although the culprits were never discovered, it is extremely unlikely that Alcibiades, for all his wild ways, had anything to do with the outrage.

opera forensi. At Rome this would normally mean 'by his services on their behalf as a barrister in the law courts'. At Athens anyone involved in a lawsuit had to speak for himself. *Forensi* must therefore be understood in a wider sense 'by his political services'.

suos reddiderat: 'he had made his own'. For this use of *reddo*, cf. French *rendre* and English *render*.

6. **in domo sua:** see note II. 1.

mysteria. A parodying of the Eleusinian mysteries is meant. Eleusis was a small town in Attica twelve miles

E

WNW. of Athens.   Here the cult of Demeter, Persephone and Dionysus was practised, which offered to its initiates the promise not merely of survival but also of happiness after death.   Those who had been initiated were not allowed to divulge the ceremonies they had witnessed, much less to parody them.

coniurationem: 'a political conspiracy'.   Alcibiades and other wealthy young aristocrats with whom he associated were suspected by many of wishing to overthrow democracy at Athens and set up an oligarchy.   Later in the war two short-lived oligarchies were in fact established. Their outrageous behaviour convinced the Athenians that democracy in spite of its faults was much to be preferred.

IV

1. **in contione.**   As Athens was literally a democracy, the assembly of the people had full power to take whatever action it thought fit.

compellabatur.   Note the tense.   The accusation was made on more than one occasion.

tempus . . . proficiscendi.   In Latin one noun depending on another is genitive.   English uses various prepositions: here 'the time *for* setting out'.

agi: *agere* is commonly used, as here, of legal action.

de praesente: sc. *se*.   This form of the ablative singular of a present participle is normal in the ablative absolute construction, but elsewhere rare.

invidiae crimine: 'a charge which was the outcome of mere spite'.

2. **quiescendum:** sc. *esse sibi,* 'that they must keep quiet'.

noceri: sc. *ei.*   Being a dative verb, *noceo* can only be used impersonally in the passive.

quo is exisset: *quo* is ablative of 'time when'.   Its antecedent is *tempus.*   *exisset* is subjunctive merely because it is inside indirect speech.   It replaces a future perfect indicative in the original words.

3. **quod sacra violasset.** The subjunctive shows that this is not stated by the historian as a fact: it is merely what Alcibiades' enemies were alleging.

reum fecerunt: *reus* is 'a defendant in a lawsuit'. Tr. 'they brought a charge against him of having . . .'

a magistratu: here used in a collective sense. The decisions of the sovereign people were carried out by ten Generals, elected annually.

ut domum rediret: an Indirect Command, following *nuntius*.

provinciae: used in its original non-geographical sense of the task assigned to a consul, general, etc., the sphere in which he exercised his *imperium*.

erat: with *missa*.

4. **inde:** 'from there' rather than 'afterwards'.

5. **capitis damnatum:** 'condemned to death'. A genitive is used with verbs of accusing and condemning to define the nature of the charge or punishment. It depends on a cognate accusative which can be understood out of the verb, viz. *accusationem* or *damnationem*.

usu venerat: 'had actually happened'. This curious phrase is not uncommon. *Usus* here signifies 'practical experience', 'what one encounters in real life'. Cf. VI. 3.

Eumolpidas. According to legend Eumolpus was a Thracian priest who introduced the Eleusinian mysteries (see note III. 6) into Attica. The Eumolpidae of classical times claimed to be his descendants, and were a family of hereditary priests in charge of the mysteries.

ut se devoverent: *se* refers back to Alcibiades, the subject of *audivit* which introduced the Indirect Statement.

quo testatior esset. A purpose clause containing a comparative adjective or adverb is introduced by *quo* in place of *ut.* *quo* = *ut eo* 'in order that by this action'.

6. **consuerat:** contraction for *consueverat*.

nam . . . paruisse. Latin will drop into indirect speech on the slightest excuse. Here the parenthetic *ut* *ipse praedicare consuerat* is sufficient justification for a reported version of Alcibiades' remarks.

plusque . . . paruisse: 'and had paid more attention to their own anger than to the interests of the state'.

7. Deceleam . . . tenuerunt. In the early years of the war the Spartans and their allies had invaded Attica each spring, remained for a few weeks doing as much damage as they could, then gone home. Now on Alcibiades' advice they established a permanent fortress some fifteen miles north of Athens, thereby cutting the short overland route from Euboea where the Athenians had kept their flocks and herds since the beginning of the war. This made it necessary to import all food by sea.

Ioniam a societate averterunt Atheniensium. The Ionians, i.e. the Greeks living along the central part of the west coast of Asia Minor and in the nearby islands, were tempted by Athens' heavy losses in Sicily to try to gain their independence. In response to appeals for help the Spartans sent them a fleet in 412 B.C. Alcibiades accompanied the expedition as an unofficial chief of staff to the Spartan admiral, and persuaded many wavering cities to join the revolt.

V

1. ab ipsis desciceret: sc. from the Spartans. *Ipsis* has been used instead of *se* for greater clarity.

2. id Alcibiades . . . celari non potuit. The active form would be: *id Alcibiadem celare non potuerunt.* With *celare* both the thing hidden and the person from whom it is hidden are accusative; either can become the subject of a passive sentence.

ea sagacitate: ablative of quality. 'such was his shrewdness that . . .'

3. Atheniensium . . . opes senescere. Take *Atheniensium* with *opes, male gestis . . . rebus* being ablative absolute, 'after the Sicilian disaster' in 413 B.C.

Lacedaemoniorum crescere: supply *opes*. Sparta's progress had been greatly helped by Tissaphernes. To many Athenians it now seemed that their only hope of winning the war was for Alcibiades to persuade Tissaphernes to change sides. Hence the agitation for his recall from exile and a readiness even to abandon democracy if this would facilitate help from Persia. Alcibiades failed to bring over Tissaphernes, but the plot to set up an oligarchy was carried through in 411. After four months the Athenians returned with relief to democracy.

4. **erat enim eodem . . . sensu:** another ablative of quality: 'he shared Alcibiades' political views.'

6. **consilio:** 'tact'.

VI

1. **his:** dative with *obviam*. It is put first by way of connection, cf. connecting relative pronouns. Alcibiades' triumphal return to Athens was in May 407.

2. **eius opera:** ablative of *opera* 1. f. 'by his doing'. Cf. *quorum opera*, § 4 inf.

quod . . . expulissent: virtual indirect speech. The *quod* clause states the reason the Athenians themselves were giving. Hence the subjunctive verb.

3. **e navi.** Notice the old form of the ablative singular of an -I stem noun. Cicero uses both *navi* and *nave*.

nisi Olympiae victoribus. *Olympiae* is best taken as locative: 'victors at Olympia.' *victoribus* is near enough in meaning to a participle to explain the slight irregularity.

coronis . . . vulgo donabatur: not 'by the crowd', which would require *a* or *ab*. The ablative of *vulgus* is used adverbially to mean 'universally', 'everywhere'.

4. **astu venit:** *astu*, a Greek word meaning 'town', is used especially for Athens, just as *urbs* alone often means Rome. Cf. 'Town' and 'City' used of London. *Astu* here is accusative, the plain accusative being used for 'motion towards' as with names of towns.

nemo tam ferus . . . quin lacrumarit: one of the simpler uses of *quin*, where it merely equals *qui non*. What follows is a result clause.

5. **resacrare:** 'to remove the curse from him': a rare word, nowhere else used in this sense.

VII

1. **tota res publica domi bellique tradita:** *belli* is locative replacing the more usual *militiae:* 'the entire conduct of public affairs, both civil and military, was turned over to him.'

apud Cymen. According to Xenophon (*Hellenica* I. 5) it was a minor naval defeat off Notium, about 100 miles south of Cyme which caused the Athenians to change their minds—although Alcibiades himself was not present at the battle, being busy besieging Phocaea, not far from Cyme. In any case the reaction was inevitable. No one, not even Alcibiades, could have lived up to the exaggerated reputation (*nimiam opinionem*, § 3) which he had acquired.

minus ex sententia: lit. 'less in accordance with their opinion'. Tr. 'because his handling of the campaign had not come up to their expectations'.

3. **malo fuisse:** predicative dative: 'was for a bad thing to him', i.e. was harmful to him. Cf. *ei praesidio fuit* (Att. X. 5), 'he was for a protection to him', i.e. he protected him.

absenti: sc. *ei*, dative of disadvantage.

4. **primus Graecae civitatis:** 'was the first member of a Greek state to . . .'

barbarum: contraction for *barbarorum*.

VIII

1. **apud Aegos flumen:** at Aegospotamos, 'the Goat's River', on the north shore of the Dardanelles. Here in 405 B.C. the Spartan commander Lysander, coming across from the other side of the straits, took the Athenian fleet by surprise and captured it almost without a blow. As a result Athens was at the mercy of Sparta and capitulated the following year.

in eo: explained by the *ut* clause which follows. 'whose chief concern was to prolong the war. . . .'

Atheniensibus: dative with *erat super* (= *supererat*.)

2. **vulgo:** sc. the troops.

agere: 'to make proposals'.

Xenophon gives a different and more plausible version of this intervention. It is highly unlikely that any Thracian king could have dislodged Lysander from Lampsacus, on the other side of the Dardanelles where he was firmly established under Persian protection. Xenophon makes Alcibiades intervene merely because he realised the danger the Athenian fleet was in as it lay on an exposed shore, two miles from Sestos, the nearest friendly harbour. He urged that they should move to Sestos but his advice was treated with contempt.

eo . . . quod: 'for this reason . . . namely, because . . .'

4. **si quid secundi . . . adversi . . .:** partitive genitives. 'if anything of success' = 'if any success'.

eius delicti. Take *eius* as masculine, referring to Alcibiades: 'he alone would have to answer for Alcibiades' failure.'

5. **occasio . . . opprimendi exercitus:** 'a chance of annihilating your army'. Notice that when in English such verbal nouns have an object, in Latin the phrase is turned passive, and the gerundive is used.

6. **neque ea res illum fefellit:** better expressed passively in English: 'nor was he mistaken in this view'.

praedatum: 'to plunder'. The supine in *-um* is only used to express purpose after a verb of motion. It resembles an accusative of 'motion towards', e.g. *domum Romam*, but indicates motion towards an action instead of to a place. Cf. *nuptum dedit*, Dion I. 1.

tempus rei gerendae: 'an opportunity of striking a decisive blow.'

bellum delevit: 'he brought the war to an end'. This odd use of *delere* is found also in Cicero.

IX

1. **arbitrans:** Since this reflection preceded and was the cause of his departure, a more exact author would have

used a perfect participle. By a curious perversity, the present participles of deponents are used more freely than those of normal verbs.

penitus in Threciam: 'in the depths of Thrace.' Notice the accusative, which is logically correct.

2. **qui . . . abstulerunt . . . non potuerunt:** *qui* should be taken as a connecting relative, *abstulerunt* and *potuerunt* as co-ordinate main verbs. In Latin they are coupled by contrast, in English 'but' must be inserted.

apportarat: contraction for *apportaverat.*

3. **quinquagena talenta:** fifty talents each (sc. year), an enormous sum—say, £50,000—which is quite incredible for so obscure a place.

4. **omni ferebatur cogitatione:** 'he devoted all his attention to . . .' For *ad patriam liberandam* see note III. 1.

5. **neque dubitabat se consecuturum:** 'and he felt sure he would succeed'. Note that Nepos has not used the normal construction of *quin* and a subjunctive after a negative verb of doubting.

eius conveniundi potestatem: 'a chance of meeting him'. lit. 'of him being met'. *Convenire* takes an accusative object and can therefore be used personally in the passive.

ei bellum parare: dative of disadvantage: 'against him'.

X

1. **Critias ceterique tyranni.** The second eclipse of democracy at Athens came in 404 B.C. when Sparta had won the war. With Lysander's approval, Theramenes and Critias organised an oligarchy of thirty. In the struggle for power which followed, Critias ousted Theramenes and had him condemned to death. During their brief reign of eight months the Thirty earned the name of 'tyrants' by ruthlessly murdering hundreds of their fellow citizens.

quare . . . persequeretur: Indirect Command.

2. **accuratius sibi agendum cum Pharnabazo:** 'that he must handle Pharnabazus with greater care'.

renuntiat: not in its usual meaning of 'bring back word' but 'renounce'.

quae regi cum L. essent: 'the (Persian) king's agreement with the Spartans'.

nisi . . . tradidisset. Like *essent, tradidissent* is subjunctive only because it is a subordinate verb in indirect speech. The main clause of the condition is concealed in *renuntiat,* which equals 'said he would renounce . . . unless . . .'

3. **non tulit hunc.** If the text is correct, this must mean 'did not hear him unmoved'. *hoc* would be much easier.

violare clementiam: 'to disregard the claims of mercy'.

4. **vicinitati.** Take the dative with *dant negotium.* The abstract noun is used for the inhabitants of the district.

quem: for *eum, quem.*

5. **vestimentorum:** partitive genitive with *quod:* 'all the clothes which . . .'.

flammae vim: 'the fierce flame(s)'. Cf. *altitudines montium* for 'lofty mountains'.

6. **contectum . . . mortuum:** sc. *Alcibiadem.* The introduction of *mortuum* and the contrasted *vivum* is highly artificial.

diem obiit supremum. Here we have this euphemism for dying in its full form; often *obiit* is used alone, or, as in Dion X. 3, *supremum* is omitted.

annos circiter XL natus. He must have been at least forty-five.

XI

1. **gravissimi historici:** 'historians whose opinions carry great weight'.

maledicentissimi. As the works of Theopompus and Timaeus have not survived, we cannot be sure which two are meant. The description, however, can scarcely apply to Thucydides.

2. **praedicarunt:** for *praedicaverunt*. Obviously each of these statements would not be found in all three historians. Nepos is here combining their information.

3. **adeo . . . inservisse:** 'devoted himself so intensively to . . .'

ingenii acumini. The stupidity of Boeotians was proverbial at Athens.

inserviunt. Note the indicative. This clause, like *quorum . . . ponebatur* below, is not part of the quoted words but an explanatory remark of Nepos.

4. **parsimonia victus:** 'by the frugality of his way of life'.

DION

I

1. **implicatus:** 'connected with'.

tyrannide. Note that *tyrannus* means 'monarch', 'absolute ruler', not necessarily 'tyrant'.

quarum priorem . . . Dioni. Greek custom permitted the marriage of a half-brother and half-sister and also of an uncle and niece. For *nuptum dedit* see note on Alc. VIII. 6.

2. **multa alia bona:** 'many other good qualities'.

3. **intimus:** 'a close friend'.

salvum . . . studebat: sc. *eum:* 'he was anxious that no harm should befall him'. An accusative with *studere* is rare.

4. **quae essent illustriores:** 'any which were . . .' The subjunctive (consecutive or generic) is used because no specific ones are meant.

5. **suspexerunt:** 'looked up to', 'respected'. The participle *suspectus* is the only part of *suspicere* which can have the meaning 'suspect'.

II

1. **quanto . . . ornamento.** For the predicative dative, cf. note Alc. VII. 3.

quo: causal: 'and so it came about that . . .'

2. **accerseret:** Though *arcesso* is the usual form in classical Latin, *accerso* is preferred also by Sallust.

eius audiendi cupiditate: cf. note Alc. VIII. 5.

dedit huic veniam: 'he complied with his (Dion's) wishes'.

magna . . . ambitione: 'with much pomp'. Besides its original meaning of 'going round canvassing for votes', *ambitio* can also mean 'a desire to impress others by outward show'.

3. **Dione:** ablative of comparison.

quippe quem venumdari iussisset: *quippe qui* with a subjunctive gives an explanation 'inasmuch as . . .' *venum-dare* 'give for sale', i.e. 'sell' is rare, being used only of selling human beings into slavery. *Vendere* the normal word for 'sell' is a contraction of this phrase.

4. **quo cum gravi conflictaretur:** *gravi* agrees with *quo* sc. *morbo.* The cause of the illness is said to have been excessive celebrations when the Athenians awarded first prize to the play which Dionysius had entered for the Lenaean festival in 367.

quem ad modum se haberet: 'how he was'.

si forte maiori esset periculo. In spite of the position of *ut,* this condition is inside the Indirect Command. Hence the subjunctive verb. Take *maiori periculo* as predicative dative, with *morbus* as the subject of *esset:* 'in case it should become more dangerous'.

quod . . . putabat. The indicative verb shows that this is an explanation inserted by Nepos.

5. **agendi . . . potestas:** 'an opportunity for negotiations'.

aeger: 'the invalid', inserted to mark the change of subject. Notice the order: *hoc* stands first as a connecting word.

ut somno sopitus: 'as if he had fallen asleep'.

III

1. **qui vellet:** cf. note on *iussisset* (II. 3). This time the usual *quippe* has been omitted.

morem ei gessit: lit. 'did his way', or, as we should say, 'let him have his way'.

2. **in eo libro.** This book (by Nepos) has not survived.

IV

1. **amore populi:** 'popularity'. The genitive is subjective, i.e. if *amore* were turned into a verb, *populi* would become its subject.

daret: Dionysius is the subject: 'afraid of giving him (Dion) an opportunity of overthrowing him (Dionysius).' Opinion is divided about such phrases as *sui opprimendi*: but as no Roman would write *sui opprimendorum* if the subject were plural, it seems best to consider *opprimendi* as a gerund and *sui* as part of *suus*, not gen. of *se*, i.e. 'of his overthrow' not 'of him being overthrown'.

utriusque causa: 'for the sake of both of them'.

inter se. Having no pronoun for 'one another', Latin uses this phrase.

2. **invidiae:** see note on *malo* (Alc. VII. 3): 'it was causing much ill feeling against the tyrant'.

4. **sobrio:** sc. *ei*: 'in which he was sober'.

5. **vitae statum commutatum:** 'the change in his way of life'. Cf. *castra capta* 'the capture of the camp', *ab urbe condita* 'from the foundation of the city'.

illuc revertor: sc. to the point in his narrative which Nepos had reached in § 2, before the digression about Dion's son.

V

2. **magnarum opum putabatur:** sc. *esse*. *opum* is a genitive of description: 'was considered to be very strong'.

3. **maximo animo . . . oppugnatum:** 'courageously setting out to attack with two merchant ships a power of

50 years' standing . . .' Distinguish *oppugnatum*, a supine expressing purpose, from *munitum* a perfect participle passive.

decem equitum: sc. *milibus*.

quod . . . est visum: parenthetic 'a feat which astounded the world'.

adeo facile perculit: sc. *imperium*.

Siciliam attigerat. He landed at Heraclea Minoa on the south-west coast of Sicily, about 120 miles west of Syracuse. On his way to Syracuse volunteers flocked to join him (cf. *odio tyranni*). Plutarch says there were 5000, Diodorus 50,000!

ex quo intellegi potest. Note Nepos' eagerness to point a moral. Cf. IX. 5.

4. in Italia classem opperiebatur. If this seems off the direct route from Corinth to Syracuse, it should be remembered that Greek sailors, having no compass, preferred to remain in sight of land. Though twice as long, they would normally choose the coasting voyage via Corcyra and the heel of Italy rather than sail due west across the open sea. Dion had risked the direct crossing.

quae res . . . fefellit: 'in this he was mistaken'.

5. regios spiritus: a difficult phrase. Its natural meaning is 'royal arrogance' but that would be an attribute of Dionysius, not his subjects. *Spiritus* here seems to be used for *animi* in the sense of 'feelings', 'disposition' towards a person. Tr. 'their feelings (of loyalty) towards their king'.

urbis Syracusarum. The apposition is normal, as in *urbs Roma*.

praeter arcem et insulam. Ortygia, an island about one mile long and less than half a mile wide, divided the two harbours of Syracuse. Its northern end had been connected to the rest of the city by a mole, which had now been removed, probably by Dionysius I. Although lower than the rest of Syracuse, it was called the citadel because of its naturally strong position.

6. 'brought the matter to this point, that . . .' lit. **eo:** adverb, explained by the following *ut* clause.

obtineret. Peace terms are regarded as instructions, and when reported become Indirect Commands.

Italiam: sc. that part of Italy which was under Syracusan rule, the southern peninsula as far as Thurii.

uni: with *cui*: 'the one man in whom . . .'

VI

1. **sua mobilitate:** 'with her usual fickleness'.

quem: for *eum quem*. If the antecedent is some part of *is*, it is usually omitted when the relative clause precedes the main clause, especially if, as here, the two pronouns would be in the same case.

demergere: a metaphor from the setting sun.

adorta: *adoriri* with infinitive, meaning 'set about doing something' is rare in Cicero but common in Livy.

2. **parens:** in apposition to the subject of *accepit*. Note the brevity of the Latin. We might say 'the heaviest blow a parent can suffer'.

3. **quod . . . non concedebat:** 'because he did not acquiesce in Dion's supremacy'.

4. **rhapsodia:** a Greek word, not found elsewhere in Latin. It means (1) epic poetry, (2) a portion of epic poetry long enough for a single recitation, e.g. a book of Homer's *Iliad* or *Odyssey*. The quotation is from *Iliad*, II. 204.

5. **obsequio:** 'by showing consideration for others'.

interficiundum curavit: 'had him murdered'. The gerundive in *-undus* is an archaism. According to Plutarch Dion merely connived at the murder.

VII

1. **adversus se sensisse:** *sentire* is frequently used of political views. Cf. *cum Caesare sentire* 'to support Caesar', Cic. *ad Att.* VII. I. 3.

2. **neque, quo manus porrigeret, suppetebat.** The subject of *suppetebat* is the understood antecedent (cf. note

VI. 1) of the relative purpose clause, 'nor was there anything for him to lay hands on'.

id: 'his dilemma'.

3. **insuetus male audiendi.** The genitive is objective,
cf. *cupidus bellandi* 'desirous of fighting'. Note that *insuetus*,
like *cupidus*, is formed from a verb which takes a prolate
infinitive. *male audire*, 'to hear (others speaking) badly (of
oneself)' is a Greek expression borrowed by several Latin
authors, including Cicero.

male existimari: object of *ferebat*. *existimari* is
impersonal: 'that a low opinion of him should be held by
those . . .'

quorum: with *laudibus*.

offensa in eum militum voluntate: 'when the
sympathies of his troops had turned against him'. Nepos
has omitted to give any reason for their changed attitude.

VIII

1. **quorsum evaderent.** An Indirect Question is
occasionally used after *timere*, which then means 'to be
apprehensive about'.

sine ulla religione ac fide. The two nouns are not
synonymous. *religio* implies respect for the gods, *fides* is
good faith in one's dealings with other men.

2. **suorum negotium:** 'the handling of his affairs'.

qui se simularet . . .: subjunctive not merely
because this is a subordinate clause in indirect speech, but
because the pretence of enmity is part of the purpose of the
scheme: 'so that he might pretend'.

quem si invenisset . . .: *quem* is a connecting
relative. *invenisset* represents a Future Perfect Indicative
in the original words, 'if he found a suitable man, he (Dion)
would easily discover . . .' The subject of the infinitives,
being also the subject of *invenisset*, is omitted.

dissidentis: accusative plural, with *sensus*. *Dissidenti*
is an attractive emendation. For *sensus* cf. note on *sentire*,
VII. 1.

3. **excepit has partes:** a common metaphor from the theatre: 'assumed this part'.

coniuratione confirmat: *coniuratio* has here its original meaning 'the act of swearing together'. Tr. 'he binds them by an oath'.

4. **multis consciis quae gereretur:** ablative absolute: 'since many were aware of what was going on'.

cuius de periculo. The antecedent is *eum* (sc. Dion) understood.

5. **hac religione:** i.e. *huius iurisiurandi religione. religio* has here is literal meaning of 'something binding' 'an obligation' (from *ligare*, to bind).

prius . . . quam conata perfecisset. In the original words of his fear this verb would be Future Indicative. Notice the use of *conata* in a passive sense.

IX

1. **a conventu . . . remotum:** 'had absented himself from the gathering'.

a foribus qui non discedant. The antecedent is *certos*. The subjunctive verb shows the relative clause expresses purpose: 'with instructions not to leave the door'.

armatis ornat: 'mans with armed troops'.

2. **agitari:** 'to be kept under way'.

cogitans . . . ut haberet qua fugeret: *ut haberet* is best taken as an Indirect Deliberative Question (*ut = quo modo*); *qua* (sc. *via*) *fugeret* is the same. Cf. *quid huic responderet non habebat.* (Cic.), where the use of *quid* proves this is not a relative clause. Tr. 'working out how he might have a way of escape'.

3. **ad Dionem eant:** Indirect Command, explaining *negotium*. For the omission of *ut* cf. *velim venias*, 'I should like you to come'.

conveniendi eius gratia: 'in order to seek an audience with him'. *Causa* is more common than *gratia* in this idiom.

4. propter notitiam: 'because they were well known

5. qui . . . malunt. The antecedent is *eorum* to be understood with *vita*.

facile intellectu. Supines in -*u* are rare, and only used with adjectives. They are best explained as datives of the verbal noun: 'easy to understand' or 'for understanding'.

6. si propria voluntate fuissent: 'if they had had any personal good will (towards him)'.

telum foris flagitantes: a clumsy expression, though the meaning is clear enough. As the assassins are inside, they cannot properly be said to demand a weapon from outside—though this is precisely what we say in English.

X

1. Dioni vim allatam: 'that a violent attack had been made upon Dion'. The indirect speech follows *rumore*.

2. ab Acherunte. Strictly Acheron was only one of several rivers which were believed to flow through the underworld. This is the only instance of its being used by a prose writer for the underworld itself. Vergil, however, writes: *flectere si nequeo superos, Acheronta movebo.* The form *Acheruns* which is common in earlier writers like Plautus is another of Nepos' archaisms.

3. celeberrimo loco: The omission of *in* is normal with *loco* and *locis* when qualified by adjectives.

sepulcri monumento: lit. 'a memorial consisting of a tomb', a defining genitive.

diem obiit: see note. Alc. X. 6.

Among the few genuine ancient letters in Greek are two written by Plato to Dion's friends bitterly lamenting his murder and advising them on their future conduct. (*Epistles*, VII and VIII.)

Callicrates' plot brought him control of Syracuse but only for one year. There followed several years of disorder including a short period when Dionysius II regained

F

possession of the city.   Democracy was finally restored by
Timoleon, who is the subject of another of Nepos' *Lives*.

ATTICUS

I

1. **ab origine . . . generatus:** 'descended from one
of the most ancient Roman families'.

perpetuo.   Take this closely with *maioribus:* 'by his
ancestors in unbroken succession'.

equestrem . . . dignitatem: 'the rank of *eques*'.
There is no satisfactory English equivalent for *eques*.   In
Atticus' time a Roman *eques* had as little to do with horses
as most English knights have today.   Originally, under the
kings, *equites* were men wealthy enough to serve in the
cavalry: by the first century B.C. they were businessmen
and bankers who had acquired great wealth from Rome's
foreign conquests and had emerged as a political force with
interests quite distinct from those of either Senate or People.

2. **patre usus est.**   It is a short step from *uti* with an
abstract noun, e.g. *otio* 'to enjoy leisure', to *uti* with persons,
'to enjoy the company of', 'to associate with'.   Here it
means no more than *patrem habuit*.

ut tum erant tempora: restricts *diti* 'by the
standards of that day'.

quibus . . . impertiri debet.   The normal construction with *impertire* is to impart something (acc.) to
somebody (dat.): but, like *donare*, it can also have the
person accusative and the thing ablative.   Here we have
this construction in the passive.

3. **suavitas oris.**   The context shows that *os* here means
'mouth' in the sense of 'enunciation', 'delivery'.

quae tradebantur.   Passages either from Greek
poets like Homer and the dramatists, or from early Latin
authors like Ennius and Cato are meant.   When Atticus
went to school most of the masterpieces of Latin literature
had still to be written.

nobilis ferebatur: 'he acquired a distinguished reputation'. For *ferre* in the sense 'say', 'report', cf. *homo omnium, ut ferebant, acerrimus* (Cic.)

4. **L. Torquatus, C. Marius filius, M. Cicero.** See Index of Proper Names. The sixteen surviving books of Cicero's letters to Atticus are evidence of the long friendship between the two men.

his. The sense shows this is dative, 'dearer to these' and not ablative of comparison.

perpetuo: 'throughout his life'.

II

1. **illius periculi.** After both the Gracchi had met violent deaths there had been a lull in the struggle between the tribunes of the people and the Senate for control of the State. Further fighting broke out in 100 B.C. when the elder Marius as consul obeyed the Senate and crushed his own supporters. In 88 Sulpicius, a young tribune, renewed the challenge to the Senate's supremacy, opposing in particular their choice of Sulla as commander for the war against Mithridates. Sulla at the time was in Italy with six legions. He marched on Rome, captured and killed Sulpicius and impaled his head on the rostra in the Forum.

2. **Cinnano tumultu.** As Sulla was obliged to leave at once for the East, further disorders followed at Rome with both sides massacring their opponents indiscriminately. The *populares*, led by Cinna, one of the consuls in 87, emerged as victors for the time being. By holding no elections and generally ignoring the constitution (cf. *tumultu:* 'disorder') they retained power until Sulla's return in 83.

pro dignitate: 'as befitted his rank'.

quin . . . offenderet: 'without falling foul of one side or the other'. For the construction see note Alc. VI. 4.

obsequendi: depends on *tempus*. See note on *tempus proficiscendi*, Alc. IV. 1.

Marium hostem iudicatum. When Sulpicius was killed by Sulla in 88, both the Marii had escaped. In their absence they were proclaimed public enemies, i.e. they lost all their rights as Roman citizens, their property was confiscated and they could be killed with impunity.

cuius fugam . . . sublevavit: 'whom he helped . . . during his exile'.

3. **illa peregrinatio.** Atticus' travels (not Marius'). In the prevailing anarchy Atticus showed typical prudence in transferring his capital to Greece.

4. **gratiam:** 'personal charm', a rare meaning in classical prose.

versuram facere: 'to raise a loan'; lit. 'to make a turning, or change' sc. of one's creditors, by contracting new debts in order to pay off old.

neque . . . haberent: 'and could not do so on reasonable terms'.

se interposuit: 'he stepped in'.

5. **salutare.** When Greece was incorporated in the Roman empire in 146 B.C. Athens and one or two other famous cities were allowed a large measure of self-government out of respect for their past achievements. We have several references to their incompetent administration of their affairs, especially their finances.

III

1. **par:** 'their equal'.

huic . . . honores . . . haberent: *habere* is regularly used for 'holding' various kinds of function, e.g. *senatum*, *comitia*, *delectum.* By *honores* are here meant ceremonies at which the honours were conferred. Tr. 'conferred every honour . . . on him'.

civem facere. It was a long established Athenian custom to grant honorary citizenship to benefactors or potential benefactors of their city.

2. **Phidiae:** the agent through whom Atticus conducted his business with them, as the following words explain. Lambin's conjecture *Piliae* (Atticus' wife) is at first sight

very attractive—until one realises that she married Atticus nearly ten years after he left Athens.

locis: for the omission of *in* see note Dion X. 3.

actorem auctoremque: 'agent and adviser'. The jingle must be intentional.

3. **illud . . . hoc . . .** Supply *erat* in each wing of the sentence.

in qua domicilium . . . esset: a difficult subjunctive. It may be expressing the idea which Fortune had in mind in arranging for A. to be born at Rome ('virtual indirect speech'); but it looks more like a confusion with such phrases as *non is sum qui hoc faciat*, 'I am not the sort of man to do this' (consecutive subjunctive).

ut eandem . . . haberet: 'with the result that . . .'

antiquitate: not, of course, true, though Nepos no doubt wrote it in good faith.

quae . . . praestaret: attracted into the subjunctive by *contulisset*.

unus . . . carissimus. Notice this use of *unus* to strengthen a superlative.

IV

1. **ex Asia Sulla decedens.** From 87 to 84 B.C. Sulla had been fighting Mithridates, King of Pontus. After driving him out of Greece he had compelled him to surrender the Roman province of Asia and return to his own kingdom. By that time events in Rome urgently needed Sulla's attention.

appareret: 'it was plain'.

2. **cum quibus:** with *arma ferrem*. Atticus' remark defies translation into a single English sentence. Tr. 'I left Italy in order not to side with those men in fighting you. Do not press me to return to fight against them.' Nepos does not conform to the common classical practice of writing *quibuscum*, *quocum*, etc., cf. V. 3.

officio: sc. his service in not joining Sulla's opponents.

3. **urbana officia:** sc. services in Rome which his friends might reasonably expect of him.

4. **ad comitia eorum:** 'to support them when standing for election'.

res maior acta est: a euphemism: 'some serious misfortune befell them'.

Ciceroni . . . periculis. Cicero's perils sprang ultimately from Catiline's conspiracy in 63. As consul Cicero had suppressed what might have been a dangerous revolution, but allowed the ringleaders to be put to death without trial or right of appeal. Four years later Caesar, Pompey and Crassus, finding Cicero unco-operative, allowed a bill to be introduced outlawing anyone who had caused a Roman citizen to be put to death without trial. Cicero retired to Greece where he spent a wretched year, utterly disillusioned. Having learnt his lesson he was allowed back.

HS: here for *sestertium* (gen. pl). The symbol is merely a modification of II and S (= *semis*, half), 2½ *asses* being the original value of the *sestertius*. Lewis and Short (1879) give its value as 2¼d. Today we might call it roughly 1s.

5. **tranquillatis rebus Romanis.** Conditions at Rome were less chaotic in 65 B.C. (*Cotta et Torquato consulibus*) than when Atticus first moved to Athens: but there was not to be anything approaching tranquillity until Octavian won the Second Civil War thirty-four years later.

desiderii futuri dolorem: 'its grief at the loss it was to endure'.

V

2. **pietatis.** The Romans set great store by this virtue, which may be defined as doing one's duty, especially to one's relatives and one's country. Tr. 'sense of duty'.

adoptavit. The adoption of adults was a common practice among the Romans. As its main object was to designate an heir, the adopters would normally be childless persons. Those adopted were frequently already related as here. Cf. Julius Caesar's adoption of his great nephew Octavius, also done *testamento*.

ex dodrante. The *dodrans* was ¾ of an *as* (Roman copper coin), so this phrase means '(heir) to three-quarters of his property'.

centies~sestertium: sc. *centena milia*, i.e. 10,000,000 *HS*. The omission was normal between the numeral adverb and *sestertium* which is gen. pl. depending upon the understood *milia*. Without this convention, expressing large sums of money in Latin would have been cumbersome because of the small value of a sesterce.

3. **erat nupta soror Attici . . .** We gather from Cicero's letters that Pomponia's marriage to his younger brother was an unusually stormy one.

ut iudicari possit: for Nepos' fondness for moralising cf. Dion V. 3.

4. **principatum eloquentiae.** Hortensius, who was some years senior to both Cicero and Atticus was acknowledged to be the leading Roman orator until 70 B.C. when Cicero successfully prosecuted Verres for his infamous conduct when governing Sicily. From then on there was friendly rivalry between the two, with Cicero gradually taking the lead. In politics they usually seem to have thought alike.

nulla intercederet obtrectatio: i.e. neither Cicero nor Hortensius made any unfriendly criticisms of his rival.

VI

1. **optimarum partium:** partitive genitive: '(a member) of the aristocratic (i.e. senatorial) party'. In a famous passage (*pro Sestio* 45) Cicero defines the *optimates* as 'all men who are neither criminals (*nocentes*), nor rogues by nature, nor mentally unbalanced (*furiosi*), nor involved in domestic difficulties'.

his: sc. *civilibus fluctibus*, the stormy waters of a political career.

2. **honores:** here, as usual, means 'political office'.

cum ei paterent . . .: concessive.

gratiam: probably 'influence' for the Romans saw nothing immoral in 'pulling strings': or, as in II. 4 it may mean 'personal charm'.

more maiorum: 'as in the good old days' before corruption had become rampant.

conservatis legibus: ablative absolûte: 'without breaking the law'.

ambitus: 'going round' to seek support for oneself or one's friends at an election had become a euphemism for bribery. According to Livy, the first law against it was passed as early as 433 B.C. Neither this law nor its various successors could stop the practice.

e re publica: 'for the good of the state'.

3. ad hastam publicam. A spear was symbolically stuck in the ground at all state auctions. The custom began when booty captured in battle was being auctioned, the spear indicating to passers-by the nature of the sale. Later the property of proscribed persons (see note X. 2) and the right to collect public revenues, especially provincial taxes, were auctioned in this way. By this crude system the State obtained its revenues without the trouble of collecting them: the contractors (*mancipes*) then helped themselves to as large a profit as they could. At the time of the auctions payment of the contract price had to be guaranteed by a third party as surety (*praes*).

subscribens: sc. signing the accusation when someone else had initiated the prosecution.

iudicium nullum habuit: sc. as prosecutor. This merely repeats in more general terms the two previous statements.

4. multorum consulum . . . This sentence might have been more clearly expressed. The general sense is that although many prospective governors of provinces offered him responsible positions on their staffs, A. always declined. Under the Republic, governors used to choose their staffs from amongst their friends. In most cases both looked forward to fat pickings at the provincials' expense. Cf. *rei familiaris fructum.* The poet Catullus who failed to make a fortune on Memmius' staff in Bithynia is able to make a joke of his disappointment (Cat. 10).

legati locum: the position of deputy governor, the highest post Quintus could offer him in Asia.

5. **suspiciones criminum:** 'the fears that charges might be made against him'. In theory any official returning from a province was liable to prosecution for appropriating what did not belong to him (*rerum repetundarum*). In fact these prosecutions had become such a forlorn hope that the provincials brought them against only the most flagrant offenders. More formidable were the charges made by the tax-collecting companies against governors or staff who had tried to protect the unfortunate provincials from their depredations.

eius observantia: subjective genitive: 'the courtesy which A. showed them'.

officio: a service done with no ulterior motive, solely from a sense of what is due to the recipient, e.g. a host's concern for the comfort of his guest.

VII

1. **aetatis vacatione:** 'exemption from military service on grounds of age'. Men over 46 were not called up.

quae . . . opus fuerant: 'what had been required'. N. might equally well have written *quibus opus fuerat*.

coniunctum: 'with whom he was closely connected'. Like *familiaris*, this term can be used of friends as well as relations.

non offendit. The two main clauses are coupled by contrast. Cf. Alc. IX. 2 and note.

2. **quorum partim:** *partim* is substituted somewhat awkwardly for *pars*. This use with a genitive, however, is not uncommon.

summa cum eius offensione: an objective genitive: 'thereby deeply offending him'.

3. **privatis pecunias imperaret.** The direct object of *imperare* is usually an *ut* clause; but sometimes, as here, it can be more conveniently expressed by an accusative noun.

sororis filium: young Quintus Cicero, son of Cicero's brother Quintus and Atticus' sister Pomponia.

ex Pompei castris. After Caesar's victory at Pharsalus (48 B.C.) most of the survivors on Pompey's side surrendered in a body and were pardoned by Caesar.

vetere instituto: sc. his long established policy of not taking sides.

VIII

1. **Brutos.** Marcus Iunius Brutus (later referred to by N. merely as Brutus) and Decimus Iunius Brutus (no direct relation) were, with Cassius, the leaders of the young senators who murdered Caesar in the senate house in 44 B.C. Disillusioned when they found how little enthusiasm their exploit aroused, the 'Liberators' were quickly disposed of by Antony and Octavian. The Battle of Philippi in 42 made it clear that whoever was to control Rome in future, it would not be the Senate.

2. **principem consilii:** 'his principal adviser'.

3. **excogitatum est . . . .** Strictly the *ut* clause is the subject. Tr. 'a scheme was devised for a special fund to be established . . .'

appellatus est . . .: 'an appeal was made to A. to take the lead in organising this'.

4. **qui . . . existimaret . . . removisset.** The subjunctives show the relative clause is causal.

sine factione: 'regardless of their politics'.

usurum: sc. *Brutum.*

collocuturum: sc. *se.* This change of subject without either being expressed is a little clumsy. The meaning, however, is clear.

coiturum: 'take joint action'.

consensionis: abstract for concrete: 'that band of enthusiasts'.

5. **destituta tutela provinciarum.** Before his murder Julius Caesar, who was both consul and dictator, had allotted various provincial commands for the following year.

Cassius was to have Syria, M. Brutus Macedon. Six months after the murder when their cause was already foundering, Brutus and Cassius left for their provinces. They were little concerned with their responsibilities as governors (*destituta tutela*): their one object was to raise forces to resist Antony and Octavian. Then they abandoned their provinces—Cassius actually surrendered his to the Parthians in return for their support—and after concentrating their troops in Asia Minor, crossed to Europe in 42 and were decisively defeated at Philippi.

dicis causa: a legal phrase: 'for form's sake', i.e. in name only. Caesar was not able to make his allocation effective.

6. **muneri:** purpose dative: 'for a gift'. Cf. the common abbreviation on dedicatory inscriptions D.D. (*dono dedit*).

in Epiro absens: emphasises that A. was taking no part in the struggle.

eo magis: with *adulatus est:* 'more for that reason', sc. because he was known to have helped Brutus.

IX

1. **bellum gestum apud Mutinam.** Early in 43 B.C. Decimus Brutus, whom Caesar had nominated as governor of Cisalpine Gaul, was besieged by Antony in Mutina, a town in that province, along the *Via Aemilia*. The Senate declared Antony a public enemy and after fierce fighting succeeded in raising the siege. Antony withdrew to Narbonese Gaul to collect more troops.

minus quam debeam praedicem: 'I should be guilty of an understatement'.

agitur: *agere* here means 'disturb', usually expressed by its frequentative form *agitare*.

2. **consecuturos:** For the omission of *se*, cf. *collocuturum* (VIII. 4).

omnibus rebus: ablative of separation.

liberos exstinguere: a bold metaphor. It seems more appropriate to Tacitus, but is used also, occasionally, by Cicero.

3. **Ciceronis.** Although Cicero had not been taken into their confidence by the 'Liberators', he was overjoyed at the murder of Caesar and at once threw himself into the struggle to revive the Republic. At this time he was delivering a series of speeches (his Philippics) attacking Antony in such violent language that later they cost him his life.

quibus rebus: for *eis rebus quibus*. See note, Dion VI. 1.

4. **ea tribuit ut . . .:** 'such was the assistance he gave that . . .'

proficisci: 'proceed from', i.e. be supplied by.

stiterit vadimonium: a legal technical term meaning to appear in court to answer a charge, having previously deposited bail (*vadimonium*); lit. 'to make one's bail stand'.

sponsor . . . fuerit. Atticus is the subject.

5. **emisset in diem.** She had arranged to buy the estate and a 'completion date' had been fixed when payment was to be made.

versuram facere: see note II. 4.

sine ulla stipulatione: sc. about repayment.

maximum existimans quaestum . . .: 'thinking it was an ample reward that the world should see he remembered (his friends) and could show his gratitude'.

6. **quae cum faciebat.** One of the comparatively rare cases of a *cum* clause expressing purely time. If there is the slightest suggestion of cause, the verb is subjunctive, whenever the main verb is past.

temporis causa: 'from ulterior motives'; lit. 'because of the time', i.e. the circumstances. Without being cynical, one may doubt whether Atticus' generosity was so completely disinterested. Antony, in spite of his defeat at Mutina, was still a power to be reckoned with: and this help to Fulvia would have been money well spent if he should prove the winner after all.

7. **sensim:** lit. 'perceptibly' (from *sentire*) as opposed to 'suddenly'. Here it suggests that the critics instead of suddenly presenting their complaints worked round to them gradually.

sui iudicii: genitive of quality: 'a man of his own judgment', i.e. who made up his mind for himself.

potius . . . intuebatur quam . . .: 'considered what it was right for him to do rather than . . .'

X

2. **ad adventum imperatorum:** 'just before the arrival of the generals'. Cf. *ad vesperum* 'towards evening'. The generals were Antony, Lepidus and Octavian who had now (Summer 43) joined together to form the First Triumvirate. Their combined forces greatly outnumbered those of D. Brutus in Cisalpine Gaul. His men deserted: he himself was captured and killed while trying to reach Brutus and Cassius in Asia Minor. The Senate, having no troops in Italy, was powerless to resist the 'Three' who now advanced on Rome with their armies.

proscriptionem. The names of their enemies were published by the 'Three' (*proscribere:* 'to write up in public'). A reward was offered for putting to death any of the proscribed: their property was confiscated and sold by auction, to raise funds for fighting Brutus and Cassius. Cicero and his brother Quintus were among the first to be proscribed. A succession of lists was issued until the number of victims totalled over 2000. Only one thing can be said in extenuation of this barbarity: it was no new idea. Sulla had first used proscription thirty-eight years before to wipe out opposition to the Senate. Antony at any rate must have appreciated the irony of using the same method now to crush the Senate.

fastigio: This word, meaning originally 'a gable end', came to be used for various 'heights' both literal and metaphorical. Here is is used of political power. In XIV. 2 it has lost the sense of 'height', and means merely 'position', 'status'.

4. **ne timeret:** indirect command.

5. **ne quod periculum . . .:** *quod* is from the indefinite adjective *qui*.

praesidio fuit: see note VII. 3.

suae . . . salutis: genitive of definition: lit. 'help consisting of saving his life'.

ab eo. Although this makes good sense with *seiunctam* (*eo* = *Gellio*), the order is slightly in favour of taking it with *velle* (*eo* = *Antonio*).

6. **prudentia:** an entirely appropriate term for the skill with which Atticus steered a safe course through so stormy a period: see note on *temporis causa*, IX. 6.

XI

1. **nihil aliud egit quam ut . . .:** 'he made it his one object to . . .'

quam plurimis: 'as many as he could', cf. *quam celerrime*. In this idiom the appropriate part of *posse* should always be supplied.

in Epirum. After being spared by Antony, Atticus had returned to his estates in Epirus.

defuerit: a consecutive subjunctive because the statement is a general one: 'no one . . . such that . . .'

2. **interitum Cassi et Bruti.** Both committed suicide in the course of the Battle of Philippi: Cassius thinking he was being attacked from the flank when the approaching cavalry had in fact been sent by Brutus to assist him, Brutus at a later stage when he realised the cause was lost.

Samothraciam: a small island (hence no preposition) in the north-eastern Aegean. Many republican survivors from Philippi had sought sanctuary there, perhaps because it was the centre of the worship of the Cabiri, an important mystery religion.

3. **temporariam:** not 'temporary' but 'dependent upon circumstances'. Cf. *temporis causa*, IX. 6.

4. **non florentibus se venditavit:** *non* negatives the whole clause.

Serviliam . . . coluerit. Her husband had been killed by Pompey in the disorders following Sulla's death in

78. Her brother Cato of Utica, an implacable foe of Julius Caesar, had committed suicide in 46 rather than accept Caesar's mercy. Now, having lost her son too, she would certainly appreciate Atticus' attention. *coluerit* is a causal subjunctive.

5. **neque ... non malebat:** 'and he always preferred'.

6. **sui cuique mores ...** Take *cuique* with *hominibus*, the use of *quisque* in apposition to a plural noun being normal: 'His own character fashions each man's fortune.' The source of the quotation is unknown. Possibly it comes from a lost comedy of Plautus or Terence. We find a similar sentiment in Plautus' *Trinummus* (II. 2, 82): *sapiens ... fingit fortunam sibi.*

plecteretur: *plēctere* is properly used of beating a slave for some offence he has committed. For Atticus the beating would be merely metaphorical. Tr. 'not to deserve censure'.

XII

1. **adulescenti Caesari:** sc. Octavian. On learning of his adoption by Caesar he followed the normal practice and assumed the name of his benefactor. Instead of Octavius, he became C. Iulius Caesar Octavianus. The name by which he is now known, Augustus, was a title conferred by the Senate in 27 B.C.

nullius condicionis non haberet potestatem: 'he might have married anyone he wished'.

eius: sc. *Attici.*

filiam. Her name was Pomponia Attica. It is astonishing that Nepos should have so little to say about Atticus' family life. This is the only reference to his daughter, who is mentioned merely in order that her brilliant marriage may reflect credit upon her father. Of his wife we hear nothing. Atticus married late, when he was fifty-four, and neither wife nor daughter seem to have played any significant part in his life.

generosarum nuptiis: dative after *praeoptaret:* 'to an aristocratic marriage'.

2. non est enim celandum. This remark suggests that Nepos was writing some time after 35 B.C. when the final rupture occurred between Antony and Octavian, and any connection with Antony would become embarrassing.

triumvir rei publicae (constituendae): the title granted to Antony, Octavian and Lepidus in 43. See note X. 2. Their power 'to reorganise the state' was to last five years.

3. sub ipsa proscriptione. When used in a time sense, *sub* with an abl. means 'during'; with an acc. 'just before' or 'just after'. For proscription see note X. 2.

ea consuetudine . . . After the Triumvirs had disposed of their enemies, they proceeded to proscribe wealthy men merely to obtain their wealth. 2000 equites were killed mainly from this motive.

4. multo elegantissimum . . . None of his poems has survived. However, since Quintilian writing about 100 years later does not even mention him in his review of Roman poets, Nepos' extravagant praise may be taken with a grain of salt.

neque minus: 'and equally'.

quem post . . . Note that the first half of the sentence has no main verb. With the connecting relative we have a fresh start.

praefecto fabrum: a military office. The *fabri* were the skilled craftsmen of the Roman army, carpenters, smiths, engineers, etc. They were organised as a separate corps under a *praefectus* appointed by the general and directly responsible to him.

absentem relatum expedivit: 'when his name had been put down in his absence A. had it removed from the list'.

5. laboriosius an gloriosius fuerit: 'brought him more worries or more honour'. The first *quod* is a connecting relative.

XIII

1. bonus pater familias. The only function of the *pater familias* with which Nepos is here concerned is the safeguarding of the family property. For his remarkable silence about Atticus as husband and father see note XII. 1.

emax . . . aedificator. Eoth epithets here imply a desire to add to one's material possessions in order to impress others. It was a common practice of the rich at this time to build expensive houses, often several houses in various parts of Italy. They also felt an urge to improve existing buildings. Cicero in his letters to Atticus often seeks his friend's advice about alterations he is proposing to make to one or other of his various *villae*.

in primis bene habitavit: 'he had an extremely fine house'.

2. **ab avunculo . . . relictam:** see V. 1-2.

ipsum enim tectum: the house itself, as distinct from the grounds in which it stood.

plus salis quam sumptus habebat: 'showed good taste rather than extravagance'.

nisi si. Neither is redundant, *commutavit* being understood with *nisi*. When *nisi* is used with its verb omitted, as here, it can mostconveniently be translated 'except'.

3. **usus est familia:** cf. *patre usus est*, I. 2 and note. *Familia* is here used in its original sense as a collective noun for the slaves (*famuli*) of the household.

si utilitate . . . mediocri: 'of the highest quality, if they are to be judged by the service they rendered; if by outward appearances, rather below average'.

pueri. Slaves of any age were referred to as 'boys'. There are not three groups of slaves but two, since *pueri litteratissimi* includes both those who read aloud and those able to copy manuscripts.

librarii. The stock which Roman booksellers carried was very limited and anyone wishing to acquire a book at all out of the ordinary would have to try to borrow a copy, and then have it transcribed by an educated slave. Atticus' *librarii* were employed in this way to increase his library; but their main occupation was to produce copies for sale. He published a great number of books by Greek authors from manuscripts he had acquired in Greece; and

G

from Cicero's letters we find it was he who published his friend's speeches and other works and constantly urged him on to fresh efforts.   Cf. *ad Att.* II. 7 where Cicero tactfully evades a pressing request for a treatise on geography.

artifices ceteri: slaves possessing various other special skills, e.g. cooks or carpenters.

cultus domesticus: 'the proper running of a house'.

apprime: used by Plautus and Terence and also by late writers.   Its classical equivalent is *in primis*.

4. **factum:** i.e. trained.

quod . . . videas: potential subjunctive: 'which you might see'.

a plurimis: 'from' expressing the source of what is being perceived of *clamor ab ea parte auditus* and *a tergo, a dextra*, etc.

continentis debet duci: 'ought to be regarded as a sign of self-control': genitive of characteristic as in *hominis est errare. Non mediocris industriae*, which replaces *non mediocriter industrii*, is a modification of this use.

5. **magnificus.**   Though normally complimentary, 'doing big things' has here a bad sense: 'pretentious', 'fond of outward show'.

ut in neutram partem conspici posset: 'so that it could not attract attention on either side'; sc. of moderation, i.e. by indicating either extravagance or niggardliness.

6. **quamquam . . . visum iri putem.**   The potential subjunctive conveys the idea of possibility which cannot conveniently be suggested by the infinitive: 'although I think it may seem . . .'

non parum liberaliter: 'with no lack of hospitality'.

terna milia peraeque in singulos menses: 'on an average 3000 HS a month'.   Cicero chaffs his friend for his careful housekeeping: *olusculis nos pascere soles (ad Att.* VI. 1).   'It is your custom to feed us on little vegetables.'

expensum sumptui ferre: *expensum ferre* is a technical term in book-keeping for entering up an item of expenditure. The dative expresses either the person to whom the money was paid, or the heading under which the item was entered. *acceptum referre* is the corresponding phrase for payment received.

7. domesticis rebus interfuimus: *domesticis* may either have its strict meaning 'relating to his *domus*', or be used in a wider sense as 'private' or 'personal'. Tr. 'gained inside knowledge of his domestic arrangements' or 'of his private affairs'.

XIV

1. acroama: 'entertainment' of any audible kind, e.g. singing, instrumental music or, as here, reading aloud from the works of some favourite author. Like *anagnostes*, the word is Greek and reminds us how much of their culture the Romans owed to the Greeks.

2. abhorrerent: consecutive subjunctive: 'of such a kind that their temperaments . . .'

in sestertio viciens: see note on *centies sestertium* V. 2. When the omission of *centena milia* became a normal practice, *sestertium*, which began as a contracted genitive plural depending on *milia*, came to be thought of as a neuter singular noun of the 2nd declension. Here we have its ablative singular.

pari fastigio: see note X. 2.

3. nullam . . . villam: an obvious contrast with Cicero who had no less than eight *villae*, in addition to his town house on the Palatine.

praeter Arretinum et Nomentanum. It was customary to refer to country estates by a neuter adjective (agreeing with *praedium* understood) formed from the name of the nearest town.

usum eum pecuniae . . . metiri: 'to measure the usefulness of money not by the amount of it, but by the way it was employed'.

XV

1. itaque . . . facilitate Only the first of these two statements is a consequence of the previous sentence.

Logic has been ignored in order to achieve rhetorical effect.

religiose promittebat: lit. 'he used to promise scrupulously', i.e. only after carefully considering whether he would be able to carry out the promise.   Tr. 'he did not lightly undertake to help'.

liberalis . . . levis: sc. *esse*.   For the genitives cf. *continentis*, XIII. 4 and note.

2. **idem . . . tanta erat cura:** *idem* (nom. masc. sing.) is inserted to heighten the contrast between his caution before making a promise and his determination in carrying it out.   *tanta cura* is ablative of quality.

agi: 'was at stake'.

3. **Catonis Marci.**   If a Roman is referred to by only two of his names and these two are his *nomen* and *cognomen*, we commonly find the *cognomen* placed first.   Cf. *Marcelli Claudi* and *Scipionis Corneli*, XVIII. 4.   The inversion of *praenomen* and *cognomen*, as here, is very unusual.

rei publicae procurationem: 'undertaking public office'.

XVI

1. **adulescens idem . . . senex:** cf. note on XV. 2.

aequalibus . . . suis: 'men of his own generation'.

3. **indicio:** predicative dative.   See note Alc. VII. 3.

sunt.   The subject is *XVI volumina epistularum,* i.e. the sixteen books of Cicero's letters to Atticus which we still possess and which were about to be published by Atticus when Nepos was writing.   They give fascinating glimpses behind the scenes into the struggle for power which was going on at Rome during Cicero's lifetime.   Their author clearly did not intend them to be published.   Indeed, some of them reveal Cicero in such an unfavourable light that it has been argued they were published to further the cause of Octavian by discrediting his republican opponents.

quae qui legat, non multum desideret . . .   The verbs are Present Subjunctive because this is virtually a remote future condition: 'whoever read them, would not have much need of a continuous history . . .'

4. **vitiis ducum:** 'the blunders of the generals'.

prudentiam quodam modo esse divinationem: 'that his foresight was tantamount to prophecy'.

vivo se: ablative absolute: 'in his lifetime'.

usu veniunt: see note Alc. IV. 5.

The greater part of this chapter seems oddly irrelevant to a 'Life of Atticus'. Nepos aware of its forthcoming publication apparently could not resist this opportunity of commending the new book.

XVII

1. **annorum nonaginta:** genitive of description, depending on *quam*.

numquam cum matre in gratiam redisse. This phrase is intentionally liable to misinterpretation. The next sentence makes the meaning clear. There had never been a reconciliation because they had never had a quarrel.

2. **ea fuisse . . . indulgentia:** ablative of description. There is a third possibility, ignored by Nepos, that some of the credit for this absence of family friction should go to the mother and sister.

3. **doctrina:** sc. the philosophy of life he had acquired from his studies. Tr. 'on principle'.

percepta habuit: 'he had grasped'. *habere* with a perfect passive participle is not uncommon in classical Latin. But it rarely comes so near to a mere auxiliary verb as here (and in XVIII. 1). Cf. *inclusum in curia senatum habuerunt*, (Cic. *ad Att.* 6, 2, 8,) 'have kept the senate shut up', not merely 'have shut it up'.

non ad ostentationem: 'not to display his knowledge.'

XVIII

1. **quam adeo diligenter habuit cognitam:** 'into which he had carried out such careful research'; see note on *percepta habuit*, XVII. 3.

magistratus ordinavit: 'gave a list of the magistrates'.

2. **suo tempore:** sc. under the year when each occurred.

subtexuit: sc. he added this genealogical information in an appendix to the main work.

3. **ut . . . enumeraverit:** a result clause, following very loosely upon the previous statement.

Iuniam familiam a stirpe. The family traced its descent back to L. Iunius Brutus who in 510 B.C. drove out Tarquinius Superbus, the last king of Rome.

quis a quo . . . cepisset. Such combinations of interrogative words are commoner in Greek than in Latin. In translating the sentence it must be reconstructed, either as a series of separate questions or by using abstract nouns, e.g. '. . . which members of the family had held office, giving their parentage and the nature and date of the office'.

4. **Marcelli Claudi:** sc. *rogatu.* For the inversion of *nomen* and *cognomen* see note XV. 3.

The earliest member of this family to distinguish himself was M. Claudius Marcellus who in 222 B.C. won the *spolia opima* by killing with his own hand the Gallic chief commanding the opposing army. The Marcellus here mentioned is probably the husband of Octavia, sister of Augustus. Their son, also named M. Claudius Marcellus, was intended by Augustus to succeed him as emperor but died at the age of nineteen.

Scipionis Corneli et Fabi Maximi Fabiorum et Aemiliorum: an example of the crossed or chiasmus order, so called from the symbol for the Greek letter *chi* (χ).

Scipio's interest in the Aemilii arose from the linking of these two distinguished families by P. Cornelius Scipio Africanus, conqueror of Hannibal in the Second Punic War, who adopted an Aemilius as his son. Subsequently known as P. Cornelius Scipio Aemilianus, he was an equally distinguished general and also gained the title Africanus for capturing and finally destroying Carthage in 147 B.C.

The most famous member of the Fabii was Q. Fabius Maximus. Appointed dictator after Hannibal's crushing victories early in the Second Punic War, he restored Roman morale by his change to guerilla tactics.

5. poeticen: a Greek word in its Greek accusative form.

ceteros praestiterunt: *praestare* in the sense of 'to surpass' is not used as a trans. verb by either Cicero or Caesar. It occurs, however, in other writers and is a favourite expression of Nepos.

It should be noticed that though their subject-matter and conciseness are praised, we are told nothing of the poetic merits of Atticus' verses. He seems to have chosen singularly intractable material.

6. sub singulorum imaginibus. Atticus composed short biographies in verse to be inscribed on the bases of busts of distinguished ancestors. It was a Roman custom to display such busts in a prominent position in the *atrium*.

de consulatu Ciceronis: in 63 B.C. See note IV. 4. In one of his letters (*ad Att.* II. 1) Cicero says he enjoyed reading this work but found the style too plain and blunt for his liking.

XIX

1. Hactenus . . . edita . . . sunt: 'The preceding chapters were published . . . during A.'s lifetime.' As the previous chapter is hardly a satisfactory conclusion, we must assume that in his second edition N. has deleted his original ending.

reliqua persequemur: '. . . complete our account'.

supra: in XI. 6.

2. imperatoris divi. With subsequent emperors, whose deification after death became almost an automatic honour, *divus* means little more than 'the late'. But here, with Julius Caesar, it has all its original force and emphasises the impressiveness of A.'s achievement.

ceperat: 'captivated'.

dignitate pari: descriptive ablative: 'no less worthy of respect', sc. than Augustus.

3. conciliarit: contraction for *-averit:* 'and has won for him what no Roman citizen has hitherto been able to achieve'—not merely absolute power, like Caesar, but also the grateful acceptance of it by his fellow citizens. The sentence is strictly irrelevant but was obviously inserted to please Augustus.

4. **ex Agrippa.** For his marriage to A.'s daughter see XII. 1. Shortly after N.'s death the marriage was dissolved by order of Augustus so that Agrippa could marry the emperor's daughter Julia.

Ti. Claudio Neroni: the son of Augustus' wife Livia Drusilla by a former husband. He was subsequently the emperor Tiberius (having also been required to divorce his wife and marry Julia).

XX

2. **Attico frueretur:** 'enjoyed A.'s company'.

nullus dies temere intercessit: *temere* usually means 'rashly', 'carelessly': here it may be translated 'without some good reason'.

3. **aedis Iovis Feretri.** It was in this temple that the *spolia opima* were dedicated (see note on *Marcelli Claudi* XVIII. 4). Livy (I. 10) says this was the most ancient of all the temples at Rome and derives the title from *ferre*, 'to whom the spoils are brought'. Propertius (IV. 10. 45) connects it more plausibly with *ferire*, 'because one general smites the opposing general with his sword'.

detecta: 'having lost its roof'.

eam reficiendam curaret: *curare* is frequently used with accusative and gerundive meaning 'to have something done'.

4. **neque vero a M. Antonio . . . colebatur:** 'nor was M.A. any less attentive a correspondent when they were apart'.

curae sibi haberet. *Curae* is a predicative dative: lit 'he held it for a care to himself to inform', i.e. 'he made a point of informing'.

5. **hoc quale sit:** 'the nature of this achievement' in maintaining his friendship with both Octavian and Antony.

quantae sit sapientiae . . .: 'how much tact is required to maintain friendly relations with men who were divided not merely by . . .' For the genitive cf. *non mediocris industriae*, XIII. 4 and note.

obtrectatio: 'mutual disparagement'.

XXI

2. **medicina:** sc. *arte.* We should say 'he had never required a doctor'.

tenesmon: a Greek accusative, this being a Greek medical term.

3. **quos ex curatione capiebat:** 'those he suffered in the course of (lit. arising out of) the treatment'.

tanta vis morbi . . . prorupit: a military metaphor: 'the disorder attacked . . . so violently'. He was probably suffering from cancer of the intestine.

4. **in dies:** used instead of *cotidie* if there is a comparative adjective or adverb in the clause, or as here a suggestion of increase or decrease.

5. **quibus:** a connecting relative pronoun, referring to *vos* in the previous sentence: 'since I have satisfied you . . .'

nihil reliqui fecisse: a partitive genitive: 'I have left nothing undone'.

reliquum est ut egomet mihi consulam. As an Epicurean, Atticus considered pleasure the main object of life. His incurable illness offered only the prospect of endless pain. He had therefore calmly decided to end a life which in his opinion was no longer worth living.

6. **mihi stat:** 'I have made up my mind to . . .'

XXII

1. **ex domo in domum:** 'from one house to another'. Prepositions are omitted with *domus* only when it has the sense of 'home'.

2. **temporibus superesse:** *tempora* is frequently used, without any adjective, for dangerous or unpleasant times. Tr. 'to survive the danger'.

precis depressit: *precis* is accusative plural.

3. **Cn. Domitio C. Sosio consulibus:** in 22 B.C.   By his antiquarian researches A. himself had established that Rome was founded in the year known to us as 753 B.C. Yet even when they had this obvious fixed point from which to date events, the Romans almost always preferred to do it by the names of the two consuls for the year.

4. **sine ulla pompa funeris:** 'without any formal procession of mourners'.   It was usual for a funeral procession to be accompanied by torchbearers, even if it took place in daylight, and to be preceded by a band playing wind instruments.

sepultus est.   Burial was still practised by the Romans; but it is more likely that N. has used the word loosely for depositing the ashes in the family vault after cremation.

iuxta viam Appiam.   The Twelve Tables forbade burial inside the city.   The majority of tombs were along the great roads leading out of Rome, especially the Appian Way.   They began at the city gates and spread further and further out as the years went by.

Q. Caecili: see V. 1.

INDEX OF PROPER NAMES

All dates are B.C. unless otherwise stated.

Acheruns, -untis (*m.*): river of the underworld, usually called Acheron.

Adimantus, -i: an Athenian general.

Aegos flumen (*n.*): Aegospotamos 'the Goat's River' on north shore of Dardanelles; scene of destruction of Athenian fleet by Lysander, 405.

Aemilii, -iorum: famous Roman family.

Africanus, -a, -um: African.

Agrippa, Marcus Vipsanius (*c.* 62–12): distinguished general and lifelong friend of Augustus ; largely responsible for defeat of Brutus and Cassius at Philippi, 42, and of Antony at Actium, 31; married Pomponia, daughter of Atticus.

Alcibiades, -is (*c.* 450–404): see Life.

Andocides, -i (*c.* 440–?): Athenian orator; accused of mutilating Hermae, 415; banished but almost certainly innocent.

Anicia, -ae: cousin of Atticus, wife of Servius Sulpicius Rufus.

Antonius, Marcus (*c.* 82–30): served under Caesar in Gaul; tribune, 49; joined Caesar at outbreak of Civil War and left by him in charge of Italy; consul with Caesar 44 when Caesar murdered; after being defeated at Mutina 43, formed Second Triumvirate with Octavian and Lepidus; in East 42–31; defeated at Actium, 31; committed suicide in Egypt, 30.

Apollocrates, -is: son of Dionysius II of Syracuse; retained fortress of Ortygia when Dion captured rest of Syracuse, 357.

Appia via: Appian Way, main road south from Rome, leading to Capua, Tarentum and Brundisium; named after Appius Claudius, censor 311, who began its construction.

Arcadia, -ae (*f.*): district of Greece, in central Peloponnese.

Arete, -es: daughter of Dionysius I of Syracuse, wife of Dion.

Aristomache, -es: sister of Dion, wife of Dionysius I of Syracuse.

Arretinus, -a, -um: at Arretium, Etruscan town on upper Arno.

Asia, -ae (*f.*): Asia Minor; especially Roman province of Asia which extended over north-west part of Asia Minor.

Athenae, -arum (*f. pl.*): Athens.

Atheniensis, -e : Athenian.

Attica, -ae (*f.*): district of Greece, surrounding Athens.

Atticus, Titus Pomponius (109–32): see Life.

Bagaeus, -i: a Persian agent, sent to assassinate Alcibiades.

Balbus, Lucius Cornelius: friend of Atticus; Spaniard from Cadiz, granted Roman citizenship by Pompey; later became close friend of Julius Caesar; Cicero's speech *pro Balbo* was delivered to uphold his claim to citizenship.

Bizanthe, -es: one of Alcibiades' three forts in the Thracian Chersonese.

Boeotii, -iorum (*m. pl.*): the Boeotians; Thebes was their capital.

Brutus, Decimus Iunius: one of Caesar's legati in Gaul; a leading conspirator in Caesar's murder, 44; besieged by Antony in Mutina, 43; shortly afterwards caught and killed by Antony, while trying to reach M. Brutus and Cassius in Asia.

Brutus, Marcus Iunius (*c.* 78–42): an ardent republican; fought for Senate in Civil War; pardoned by Caesar after Pharsalus, 48 and made governor of Cisalpine Gaul; leading conspirator in Caesar's murder, 44; defeated at Philippi by Antony and Octavian, and committed suicide 42.

Byzantium, -ii (*n.*): a Greek city on west shore of south entrance to Bosphorus, later renamed Constantinople.

Caecilius, Quintus: maternal uncle of Atticus.

Caesar, Gaius Iulius (102–44): consul 59; Gallic campaigns 58–49; Civil War against Pompey and Senate 49–45; assassinated in senate by 'Liberators', 44.

Caesar, Gaius Iulius Octavianus (63–A.D. 14): great-nephew of above; born Octavius; changed name when adopted by Caesar as his heir; fought for Senate against Antony at Mutina, 43; then formed Second Triumvirate with Antony and Lepidus; gained control of Italy and western provinces after Philippi, 42; added eastern provinces when Antony defeated at Actium, 31; thereafter ruled without serious opposition by tactfully pretending Senate still supreme; given title Augustus by Senate, 27.

Calidus, Lucius Iulius: a Roman poet.

Callicrates, -is: an Athenian citizen; a member of Plato's Academy; false friend of Dion and responsible for his assassination; also called Callippus.

Canus, Quintus Gellius: a schoolfellow and lifelong friend of Atticus.

Capitolium, -ii (*n.*): the Capitol, lower of two summits of Capitoline hill in centre of Rome overlooking Forum; contained temple of Jupiter Optimus Maximus and ancient sanctuary of Jupiter Feretrius.

Cassius, Gaius: an able soldier; opposed Caesar in Civil

War and pardoned by him after Pharsalus, 48; leading conspirator in Caesar's murder, 44; committed suicide during Battle of Philippi, 42.

Cato, Marcus Porcius (95–46): Roman senator of outstanding integrity; implacable opponent of Caesar; withdrew to Africa during Civil War, where he committed suicide in Utica, after Caesar's victory at Thapsus.

Catullus, Gaius Valerius (c. 84–c. 54): one of the greatest Roman poets; wrote a variety of poems, mostly short, and strikingly sincere.

Cicero, Marcus Tullius (106–43): the great Roman orator and statesman; quaestor in Sicily, 75; made reputation as orator by prosecuting Verres, 70; consul, 63 when crushed Catiline's conspiracy; in exile 58–57; supported Pompey during Civil War but with misgivings; reconciled to Caesar, 47; retired from politics until 44; after Caesar's murder launched fierce attacks on Antony in *Philippics* 44–43; proscribed and killed, 43.

Cicero, Quintus Tullius (c. 102–43): younger brother of above; husband of Atticus' sister, Pomponia; praetor, 62; governed province of Asia 61–58; legate of Caesar in Gaul, 54; joined Pompey in Civil War but pardoned by Caesar; proscribed and killed, 43.

Cinnanus, -a, -um: of Cinna, consul, 87, and violent opponent of Sulla.

Clinias, -ae: father of Alcibiades; killed in Battle of Coronea, 447.

Corinthus, -i (*f.*): Corinth.

Cotta, Lucius: Roman consul in 65.

Critias, -ae: an Athenian politician; organised extreme oligarchy at Athens known as Thirty Tyrants, 404; overthrown after eight months.

Cyme, -es (*f.*): a town on west coast of Asia Minor.

Cyrus, -i: second son of Darius II of Persia; as governor general of Asia Minor gave great help to Lysander against Athenians; on death of Darius organised expedition of Greek mercenaries (Xenophon's Ten Thousand) in unsuccessful attempt to gain throne from his elder brother Artaxerxes; killed at Cunaxa, 401.

Darius, -ii: Darius II, King of Persia, 423–404.

Decelea, -ae (*f.*): a small town in Attica, 15 miles north of Athens.

Dion, -is (c. 408–353): see Life.

Dionysius, -ii: 1. Dionysius I, tyrant of Syracuse from 405 till his death in 367; made Syracuse the strongest power in Europe, controlling almost all Sicily and much of southern Italy. 2. Dionysius II, his son, unpopular for his misrule; lost Syracuse to Dion, 357; returned 347; finally expelled by Timoleon 344; died in Corinth.

Domitius, Gnaeus: consul in 22.

Drusilla, Livia (58–A.D. 29): wife of Tiberius Claudius Nero and mother of the emperor Tiberius; after divorce married Octavian, 38.

Elis, -idis (*f.*): a Greek city in north-west Peloponnese, near Olympia.

Epiroticus, -a, -um: of Epirus.

Epirus, -i (*f.*): a district in north-west Greece, now Albania.

Eumolpidae, -arum (*m.*): a family of priests in charge of the mysteries at Eleusis in Attica.

Fabii, -iorum: a famous Roman family.

Feretrius, -ri: cult title of Jupiter, as recipient of the *spolia opima*.

Flavius, Gaius: a friend of M. Brutus.

Fulvia, -ae: wife of Antony, her third husband; a courageous, masterful woman.

Graecia, -ae (*f.*): Greece.

Graecus, -a, -um: Greek.

Grynium, -ii (*n.*): a fortified town in Phrygia.

Hellespontus, -i (*m.*): the Hellespont, now the Dardanelles.

Heraclides, -is: a Syracusan officer banished by Dionysius II; assisted Dion to capture Syracuse; subsequently murdered after quarrel with Dion.

Herma or **Hermes, -ae** (*m.*): a Greek god; or his statue.

Hipparinus, -i: 1. Father of Dion. 2. Son of Dionysius I and Dion's sister Aristomache.

Hipponicus, -i: father-in-law of Alcibiades.

Homerus, -i: Homer, the Greek epic poet, author of the *Iliad* and the *Odyssey*.

Hortensius Hortalus, Quintus (114–50): a leading Roman orator; consul, 69; a friend of Atticus and Cicero.

Ionia, -ae (*f.*): a district of Asia Minor, in centre of west coast.

Italia, -ae (*f.*): Italy.

Iunius, -a, -um: of the *gens Iunia*, an ancient Roman family.

Iuppiter, Iovis (*m.*): Jupiter, the chief Roman god.

Karthaginienses, -ium (*m.*): the Carthaginians.

Lacedaemon, -onis (*f.*): Sparta.

Lacedaemonii, -orum (*m.*): the Spartans.

Laco, -onis (*adj.*): Spartan.

Lamachus, -i: an Athenian general; sent with Alcibiades and Nicias to conquer Sicily, 415; killed attacking Syracuse, 414.

Lucretius Carus, Titus (*c.* 99–*c.* 55): a great Roman poet; author of *de Rerum Natura*, a long hexameter poem setting out in Latin the teachings of the Greek philosopher Epicurus concerning the nature of the universe.

Lucullus, Lucius Licinius (*c.* 114–57): consul, 74; fought with great success, 74–67, in the Third Mithridatic War.

Lyco, -onis: a Syracusan.

Lycus, -i: an Athenian, father of Thrasybulus.

Lysander, -dri: a celebrated Spartan naval commander during the last years of the Peloponnesian War; destroyed Athenian fleet at Aegospotamos, 405; helped Critias establish rule of Thirty Tyrants at Athens; died fighting in Boeotia, 395.

Marcelli, -orum (*m.*)**:** a famous Roman family.

Marcellus, Gaius Claudius: consul, 50; married Octavia, sister of Augustus.

Marius, Gaius (157–86): a great Roman general; defeated Jugurtha, 105, and Teutones and Cimbri (102–101); seven times consul, but a failure as a politician.

Marius, Gaius (107–82)**:** son of above; prominent opponent of Senate; proclaimed public enemy, 88; returned from exile after Sulla's departure, 87; consul, 82; committed suicide after Sulla's victory over the *populares* at the Colline Gate.

Maximus, Quintus Fabius: consul, 45.

Mercurius, -ii (*m.*)**:** Mercury, a Roman god corresponding to the Greek Hermes.

Mocilla, Lucius Iulius: a Roman senator; fought for Brutus and Cassius at Philippi, 42.

Mutina, -ae (*f.*)**:** a town in Cisalpine Gaul, on the Via Aemilia, where Decius Brutus was besieged by Antony, 43.

Neontichos (*n.*)**:** one of Alcibiades' three forts in the Thracian Chersonese.

Nero, Tiberius Claudius (42–A.D. 37)**:** stepson of Augustus and husband of Atticus' granddaughter, Vipsania Agrippina; later the emperor Tiberius.

Nicias, -ae: an Athenian statesman and general; opposed the Peloponnesian War, and negotiated peace with Sparta, 421; opposed the Sicilian Expedition but appointed to command it with Alcibiades and Lamachus; put to death by the Syracusans, 413.

Nisaeus, -i: son of Dionysius I of Syracuse and Dion's sister Aristomache.

Nomentanus, -a, -um: at Nomentum, a Sabine town 20 miles north-east of Rome.

Olympia, -ae (*f.*)**:** a small plain in Elis, near the west coast of the Peloponnese, named from a temple there of Olympian Zeus; scene of the Olympic Games.

Orni, -orum (*m. pl.*)**:** one of Alcibiades' three forts in the Thracian Chersonese.

Pactye, -es (*f.*)**:** a town on the north shore of the Hellespont, at the east end of the Thracian Chersonese.

Peducaeus, Sextus: a friend of Atticus; praetor in Sicily, 75, when Cicero there as quaestor.

Peloponnesius, -a, -um: Peloponnesian.

Pericles, -is and **-i** (*c.* 500–429): the greatest of Athenian statesmen; his leadership was virtually unchallenged from 461 to his death; under him Athens achieved her greatest power and prosperity, and her finest artistic masterpieces.

Perses, -ae and **-is:** Persian.

Pharnabazus, -i: Persian governor of Dascylium, controlling Phrygia and Bithynia *c.* 412–393.

Phidias, -ae: Atticus' agent in his dealings with the Athenians.

Philippensis, -e: of Philippi, in Macedon, where Antony and Octavian defeated Brutus and Cassius, 42.

Philistus, -i: a Syracusan historian, and adviser of Dionysius II; wrote a history of Sicily, now lost, modelled on Thucydides.

Philocles, -s: commander of the Athenian fleet at Aegospotami, 405.

Philostratus, -i: an Athenian, brother of Callicrates.

Phrygia, -ae (*f.*): a province of the Persian empire, in north-west Asia Minor.

Piraeus, -i (*m.*): the main port of Athens, 5 miles south-west of the city.

Pisander, -dri: an Athenian politician; largely responsible for removing Alcibiades from Sicily, 415; general at Samos, 411; prominent in negotiations for recalling Alcibiades from exile and setting up a moderate oligarchy at Athens.

Plato, -onis (*c.* 427–348): a famous Athenian philosopher; a pupil of Socrates and author of many philosophical works; founder of the Academy; at Dion's suggestion twice visited Syracuse, trying unsuccessfully to turn Dionysius II into a philosopher-king; paid third visit, also unsuccessful, attempting to heal quarrel between Dion and Dionysius II.

Pompeius, Gnaeus (106–48): Pompey the Great; consul 70, 55 and 52; swept the Mediterranean clear of pirates, 67; finished Lucullus' war with Mithridates 66–63; led Senate's forces against Caesar; defeated at Pharsalus, 48, and murdered in Egypt.

Pomponius: see Atticus.

Propontis, -idis (*f.*): the Propontis or Sea of Marmora; between the Hellespont and the Bosphorus.

Proserpina, -ae (*f.*): a Greek goddess, carried off by Pluto to reign as queen of the underworld; returned each spring for six months to the world above.

Quirinalis collis (*m.*): the Quirinal, the most northern of Rome's seven hills.

Roma, -ae (*f.*): Rome.

Romanus, -a, -um: Roman.

Romulus, -i: legendary founder and first king of Rome.

Samothracia, -ae (*f.*): Samothrace, a small island in the north-east Aegean; centre of the worship of the Cabiri.

Samus, -i (*f.*)**:** Samos, an island near the west coast of Asia Minor.

Saufeius, Lucius: a Roman 'knight'; an Epicurean and a friend of Atticus.

Scipio, Quintus Cornelius Metellus: consul, 52; father-in-law of Pompey.

Servilia, -ae: sister of Cato; wife of Marcus Iunius Brutus and mother of Brutus, the 'Liberator'.

Seuthes, -is: a Thracian king and friend of Alcibiades.

Sicilia, -ae (*f.*)**:** Sicily.

Socrates, -is (469–399)**:** a famous Athenian philosopher; wrote nothing himself, but well-known to us from the works of his pupils Plato and Xenophon; accused of corrupting the young by his unorthodox views and condemned to die by drinking hemlock.

Sophrosyne, -es: daughter of Dionysius I and Dion's sister Aristomache.

Sosius, Gaius: consul in 22.

Sulla, Lucius Cornelius (138–78)**:** a ruthless champion of the Senate against the *populares*; captured Jugurtha for Marius, 106; consul, 88; won First Mithridatic War 87–83; won civil war in Italy against *populares* and began proscription, 82; dictator, 81–79; reformed the constitution for the benefit of the Senate.

Sullanus, -a, -um: of Sulla.

Sulpicius Rufus, Publius: a distant relative of Atticus; a distinguished orator; tribune, 88; joined with Marius in opposing Sulla, who marched on Rome and captured and killed him, 88.

Sulpicius Rufus, Servius: brother of above; married Atticus' cousin Anicia.

Susamithres, -ae (*m.*)**:** a Persian, sent by Pharnabazus to assassinate Alcibiades.

Syracusae, -arum (*f. pl.*)**:** Syracuse, the chief city of Sicily; founded by Corinth, 734.

Syracusanus, -a, -um: Syracusan.

Tamphilianus, -a, -um: of the Tamphili, an aristocratic Roman family.

Tarentum, -i (*n.*)**:** a Greek city on the south coast of Italy; founded by Sparta, 708.

Thebae, -arum (*f. pl.*)**:** Thebes, the chief city of Boeotia in central Greece.

Theopompus, -i: a Greek historian; born at Chios, 376; wrote a history of Greece (411–394) now lost.

Theramenes, -is: an Athenian politician; took a leading part in both attempts to establish oligarchy at Athens (411 and 404); his moderate views soon led to quarrels with the extremists; killed by Critias, 404.

Thrasybulus, -i: an Athenian naval commander at Samos, 411; led the opposition to the oligarchy set up at Athens and arranged for Alcibiades to join the democrats instead of the oligarchs.

Thrax or **Threx, -cis:** Thracian.

H

Threcia, -ae (*f.*): Thrace.
Thucydides, -is: one of the greatest of historians; an Athenian, born *c.* 460; exiled, 424, for neglecting his duties as a general; wrote an unfinished history of the Peloponnesian War (to 411) remarkable for its impartiality, its political insight and its appreciation of underlying causes.
Thurii, -iorum (*m. pl.*): a Greek city on the Gulf of Tarentum in south Italy.
Timaeus, -i (*c.* 346–*c.* 250): a Sicilian historian; author of a history of Sicily down to 264, now lost.

Tissaphernes, -is: Persian governor of Sardis, controlling Ionia, Lydia and Caria, *c.* 412–395.
Torquatus, Lucius Manlius: a school friend of Atticus; consul, 65.
Torquatus, Aulius Manlius: a friend of Atticus; fought for Brutus and Cassius at Philippi, 42.

Volumnius, Publius: a friend of Antony, in charge of his army craftsmen.

Zacynthius, -a, -um: of Zacynthus, an island off the west coast of Greece.

VOCABULARY

(*N.B.* The quantity of vowels is marked only when the syllable is naturally long.)

ā, ab (*prep.* with *abl.*)**:** from, by.

abdō, -ere, -didī, -ditum (*v.t.*)**:** hide away.

abhorreō, -ēre, -uī, -itum (*v.i.*)**:** shrink from.

abiciō, -ere, -iēcī, -iectum (*v.t.*)**:** throw away, cast down.

abrogō, -āre, -āvī, -ātum (*v.t.*)**:** terminate (an office).

absēns, -entis: absent.

abstineō, -ēre, -uī, -tentum (*v.t.*)**:** hold back.

absum, abesse, āfuī (*v.i.*)**:** be away, be absent; **tantum abesse ut . . . ut . . .:** be so far from . . . that . . .

āc (*conj.*)**:** and.

accēdō, -ere, -cessi, -cessum (*v.i.*)**:** approach.

accelerō, -āre, -āvī, -ātum (*v.t.*)**:** hasten.

accersō, -ere, -īvī, -ītum (*v.t.*) = **arcesso:** send for.

accessiō, -ōnis (*f.*)**:** addition.

accidō, -ere, -cidī (*v.i.*)**:** happen, befall.

accipiō, -ere, -cēpī, -ceptum (*v.t.*)**:** receive, understand.

accrescō, -ere, -crēvī, -crētum (*v.i.*)**:** increase.

accūrātē, -ius, -issimē (*adv.*)**:** carefully.

accūsō, -āre, -āvī, -ātum (*v.t.*)**:** accuse.

ācer, -cris, -cre: keen, shrewd.

acerbitās, -ātis (*f.*)**:** bitterness, severity.

ācroāma, -atis (*n.*)**:** entertainment.

āctor, -ōris (*m.*)**:** doer, agent.

acūmen, -minis (*n.*)**:** sharpness.

acūtus, -a, -um: sharp, quickwitted.

ad (*prep.* with *acc.*)**:** to, towards, near, according to.

adamō, -āre, -āvī, -ātum (*v.t.*)**:** love intensely.

addō, -ere, -didī, -ditum (*v.t.*)**:** add.

addūcō, -ere, -dūxī, -ductum (*v.t.*)**:** lead to, induce.

adeō, -īre, -iī, -itum (*v.i.*)**:** go to.

adeō (*adv.*)**:** to such an extent.

adferō, -ferre, -tulī, -lātum (*v.t.*)**:** bring forward.

adfinitās, -ātis (*f.*)**:** relationship (by marriage).

adhibeō, -ēre, -uī, -itum (*v.t.*)**:** apply, employ.

adhūc (*adv.*)**:** up to now.

adiungō, -ere, -iūnxī, -iūnctum (*v.t.*)**:** join to.

adiuvō, -āre, -iūvī, -iūtum (*v.t.*)**:** help, assist.

administrō, -āre, -āvī, -ātum (*v.t.*)**:** administer.

admīrābilis, -e: wonderful.

admīror, -ārī, -ātus sum (*v.t. and i.*): wonder at, admire, be surprised.

admonitus (used only in *abl. -ū*) (*m.*): advice, request.

adoptō, -āre, -āvī, -ātum (*v.t.*): adopt.

adorior, -īrī, -ortus sum (*v.t.*): attack; with *infin.:* set about.

adsum, adesse, adfuī (*v.i.*): be present.

adulēscēns, -entis (*m.*): young man.

adulēscentia, -ae (*f.*): youth.

adulēscentulus, -ī (*m.*): very young man.

adulor, -ārī, -ātus sum (*v.i.* with *dat.*): fawn upon, cringe before.

adveniō, -īre, -vēnī, -ventum (*v.i.*): arrive.

adversārius, -iī (*m.*): opponent, rival.

adversum (*prep.* with *acc.*): against.

adversus, -a, -um: turned against, adverse.

adversus (*prep.* with *acc.*): against.

advocō, -āre, -āvī, -ātum (*v.t.*): summon.

aedēs, -is (*f.*): *sing.* temple; *pl.* house.

aedificātor, -ōris (*m.*): builder.

aedificium, -iī (*n.*): building.

aeger, -gra, -grum : ill.

aemulātiō, -ōnis (*f.*): rivalry.

aeneus, -a, -um: of bronze.

aequālis, -e: equal, of same age.

aequiperō, -āre, -āvī, -ātum (*v.t.*): equal, match.

aequus, -a, -um: equal, fair, level, calm.

aerārium, -iī (*n.*): treasury, fund.

aes, aeris (*n.*): bronze, money.

aetās, -ātis (*f.*): age.

affābilis, -e: easy to speak to, approachable.

affectō, -āre, -āvī, -ātum (*v.t.*): strive after.

afferō, -ferre, attulī, allātum (*v.t.*): bring.

affīnitās, -ātis (*f.*): relationship (by marriage).

afflīgō, -ere, -īxī, -īctum (*v.t.*): strike down, afflict.

affluenter (*adv.*): affluently.

affluentia, -ae (*f.*): affluence, display of wealth.

aggredior, -dī, -gressus sum (*v.t.*): attack.

agitō, -āre, -āvī, -ātum (*v.t.*): set in motion.

agō, -ere, ēgī, āctum (*v.t.*): do, discuss, transact, disturb, make one's object.

āiō (*def. verb*): say.

aliēnō, -āre, -āvī, -ātum (*v.t.*): estrange, alienate.

aliēnus, -a, -um: belonging to another; **aes aliēnum:** debt.

aliquamdiū (*adv.*): for some considerable time.

aliquandō (*adv.*): at some time.

aliquantō (*adv.*): somewhat, considerably.

aliquī, -qua, -quod: some.

aliquis, -quis, -quid (*indef. pronoun*): someone, something.

aliquot (*indecl. adj.*): a certain number.

aliter (*adv.*): otherwise; **aliter ac:** otherwise than.

alius, -a, -ud: other, different; **aliī . . . aliī:** some . . . others.

alō, -ere, aluī, altum (*v.t.*): feed, nourish.

alter, -era, -erum: the other (of two).

alteruter, -tra, -trum: one of two.

amātor, -ōris (*m.*): lover.

ambitiō, -ōnis (*f.*): pomp.

ambitus, -ūs (*m.*): canvassing, bribery.

amīcitia, -ae (*f.*): friendship.

amīcus, -ī (*m.*): friend; **-a, -um:** friendly.

āmissus, -ūs (*m.*): loss.

āmittō, -ere, -mīsī, -missum (*v.t.*): lose.

amō, -āre, -āvī, -ātum (*v.t.*): love.

amoenitās, -ātis (*f.*): charm.

amor, -ōris (*m.*): love.

āmplitūdō, -inis (*f.*): greatness, dignity.

āmplius (*compar. adv.*): more fully, further, more.

āmplus, -a, -um: full, fine, distinguished.

an (*conj.*): or.

anagnōstēs, -ae (*m.*): reader.

animadvertō, -ere, -tī, sum- (*v.t.*): notice, realise.

animus, -ī (*m.*): mind.

anniculus, -a, -um: a year old.

annuō, -ere, -uī, -ūtum (*v.i.*): nod to, agree to.

annus, -ī (*m.*): year.

ante (*adv. and prep.* with *acc.*): before.

anteā (*adv.*): before, previously.

antecēdō, -ere, -cessī, -cessum (*v.t.*): go before, surpass.

antīquitās, -ātis (*f.*): antiquity, former times.

antīquitus (*adv.*): in ancient times.

aperiō, -īre, -uī, -tum (*v.t.*): open, reveal.

appāreō, -ēre, -uī, -itum (*v.i.*): appear, be plain.

apparō, -āre, -āvī, -ātum (*v.t.*): prepare.

appellō, -āre, -āvī, -ātum (*v.i. and t.*): call, appeal.

appōnō, -ere, -posuī, -positum (*v.t.*): place beside.

apportō, -āre, -āvī, -ātum (*v.t.*): bring.

apprīmē (*adv.*): first of all, exceedingly.

Aprīlis, -e: of April.

aptus, -a,- um: fitted, suited.

apud (*prep.* with *acc.*): at, near, with, at the house of.

arbitrium, -iī (*n.*): judgment, decision.

arbitror, -ārī, -ātus sum (*v.i.*): think, consider.

arguō, -ere, -uī, -ūtum (*v.t.*): declare, show.

arma, -orum (*n.*): arms.

armō, -āre, -āvī, -ātum (*v.t.*): arm.

arripiō, -ere, -ripuī, -reptum (*v.t.*): snatch up.

ars, artis (*f.*): art.

artifex, -ficis (*m.*): skilled craftsman.

arx, arcis (*f.*): citadel.

ascendō, -ere, -scendī, -scēnsum (*v.t.*): climb, go aboard.

asciscō, -ere, -īvī, -ītum (*v.t.*): receive, acquire.

aspergō, -ere, -ersī, -ersum (*v.t.*): sprinkle.

asperitās, -ātis (*f.*): roughness, fierceness, brusqueness.

assecla, -ae (*m.*): attendant, assistant.

astu (*indecl. noun, n.*): city, town.

at (*conj.*): but.

atque (*conj.*): and.

attendō, -ere, -tendī, -tentum (*v.t.*): stretch towards, turn towards.

attingō, -ere, -tigī, -tactum (*v.t.*): touch, reach.

auctor, -ōris (*m.*): author, adviser.

auctoritās, -ātis (*f.*): authority, initiative.

audāx, -ācis: daring.

audeō, -ēre, ausus sum (*v.t.*): dare.

audiō, -īre, -īvī, -ītum (*v.t.*): hear.

auferō, -ferre, abstulī, ablātum (*v.t.*): take away.

augeō, -ēre, auxī, auctum (*v.t.*): increase.

aureus, -a, -um: golden.

aut (*conj.*): or; **aut . . . aut . . .**: either . . . or . . .

autem (*conj.*): however.

auxilium, -iī (*n.*): help.

āvertō, -ere, -tī, -sum (*v.t.*): turn away.

avunculus, -ī (*m.*): maternal uncle.

barbarus, -a, -um: foreign, barbarian, i.e. not Greek.

bellum, -ī (*n.*): war.

bene, melius, optimē (*adv.*): well.

beneficium, -iī (*n.*): benefit, kindness.

benevolentia, -ae (*f.*): goodwill.

biduum, -ī (*n.*): a space of two days.

blandus, -a, -um: pleasant, agreeable.

bonitās, -ātis (*f.*): goodness.

bonus, -a, -um: good; *neut. pl.* = goods, property.

brevis, -e: short.

breviter (*adv.*): briefly.

C: Gaius (Roman *praenomen*); 100.

caedēs, -is (*f.*): slaughter, murder.

caelum, -ī (*n.*): heaven, sky.

calamitās, -ātis (*f.*): disaster.

callidus, -a, -um: clever, shrewd.

canō, -ere, cecinī, cantum (*v.i.* and *t.*): sing, sing of, prophesy.

capiō, -ere, cēpī, captum (*v.t.*): take, receive, captivate.

caput, -itis (*n.*): head; **capitis damnare**: condemn to death.

cāritās, -ātis (*f.*): dearness, affection.

cārus, -a, -um: dear.

casa, -ae (*f.*): cottage.

castellum, -ī (*n.*): fort.

castrum, -ī (*n.*): *sing.* fort; *pl.* camp.

cāsus, -ūs (*m.*): happening, misfortune.

causa, -ae (*f.*): cause, reason, case; **causā** (preceded by *gen.*): for the sake of.

caveō, -ēre, cāvī, cautum (*v.i.* and *t.*): beware.

cēdō, -ere, cessī, cessum (*v.i.*): yield, withdraw.

celeber, -bris, -bre: much frequented.

celer, -eris, -ere: quick.

celeriter, celerius, celerrimē (*adv.*): quickly.

cēlō, -āre, -āvī, -ātum (*v.t.*): hide; with two *accs.*: hide something from somebody.

cēnō, -āre, -āvī, -ātum (*v.i.*): dine.

centiēs (*adv.*): a hundred times.

centum: hundred.

certus, -a, -um: certain; certiōrem facio: inform.

cēterī, -ae, -a: the rest.

cibus, -ī (m.): food.

circā (prep. with acc.): around.

circiter (adv.): about.

cīvīlis, -e: of a citizen, civil, political.

cīvis, -is (c.): citizen.

cīvitās, -ātis (f.): state, citizenship.

clam (adv.): secretly.

clārē, -ius, -issimē (adv.): clearly, brightly.

clārus, -a, -um: clear, famous.

classis, -is (f.): fleet.

clēmentia, -ae (f.): mercy.

Cn.: Gnaeus (Roman praenomen).

coëō, -īre, -īvī or -iī, -itum (v.i.): go together, combine.

coepī (def. verb): begin.

cōgitātiō, -ōnis (f.): thinking, meditation.

cōgitō, -āre, -āvī, -ātum (v.i.): consider, meditate.

cognōscō, -ere, -nōvī, -nitum (v.t.): get to know, recognise.

cōgō, -ere, coēgī, coāctum (v.t.): compel.

collaudō, -āre, -āvī, -ātum (v.t.): praise highly.

collēga, -ae (m.): colleague.

colligō, -āre, -āvī, -ātum (v.t.): bind together, tie up.

colligō, -ere, -lēgī, -lēctum (v.t.): gather.

collis, -is (m.): hill.

collocō, -āre, -āvī, -ātum (v.t.): place together, give in marriage.

colloquor, -ī, -locūtus sum (v.i.): converse, discuss.

colō, -ere, coluī, cultum (v.t.): cultivate, look after.

cōmis, -e: courteous, obliging.

cōmitās, -ātis (f.): affability, courtesy.

comitium, -iī (n.): assembly; pl. election.

comitor, -ārī, -ātus sum (v.t.): accompany.

commemorō, -āre, -āvī, -ātum (v.t.): relate.

commendātiō, -ōnis (f.): commendation, excellence.

commendō, -āre, -āvī, -ātum (v.t.): commend.

committō, -ere, -mīsī, -missum (v.t.): entrust.

commoditās, -ātis (f.): advantage.

commoveō, -ēre, -mōvī, -mōtum (v.t.): move.

commūniō, -īre, -īvī, -ītum (v.t.): fortify, build.

commūnis, -e: common, approachable.

commūtātiō, -ōnis (f.): change.

commūtō, -āre, -āvī, -ātum (v.t.): change.

comparō, -āre, -āvī, -ātum (v.t.): prepare, arrange, get together.

compellō, -āre, -āvī, -ātum (v.t.): address, accuse.

comperiō, -īre, -perī, -pertum (v.t.): find out.

compleō, -ēre, -ēvī, -ētum (v.t.): fill, complete.

complūrēs, -ium: several, very many.

compōnō, -ere, -posuī, -positum (v.t.): arrange, settle.

cōnāta, -orum (n. pl.): attempt.

concēdō, -ere, -cessī, -cessum (v.t.): yield, grant, pardon.

concīdō, -ere, -cīdī, -cīsum (v.t.): cut to pieces, kill.

conciliător, -ōris (*m.*): arranger.

conciliō, -āre, -āvī, -ātum (*v.t.*): unite, arrange, bring about.

concitō, -āre, -āvī, -ātum (*v.t.*): stir up.

conclāve, -is (*m.*): room.

concupiscō, -ere, -cupīvī or **-iī, -cupītum** (*v.i.*): form a desire.

concurrō, -ere, -currī, -cursum (*v.i.*): run together.

condiciō, -ōnis (*f.*): term, condition, marriage.

condiscipulātus, -ūs (*m.*): being at school together.

condiscipulus, -ī (*m.*): fellow pupil.

cōnferō, -ferre. -tulī, -lātum (*v.t.*): bring together, contribute; **sē conferre**: betake oneself.

cōnficiō, -ere, -fēcī, -fectum (*v.t.*): finish off, kill, compose.

cōnfirmō, -āre, -āvī, -ātum (*v.t.*): strengthen, encourage.

cōnflictō, -āre, -āvī, -ātum (*v.t.*): afflict.

cōnflīgō, -ere, -flixī, -flictum (*v.i.*): fight.

cōnfluō, -ere, -fluxī (*v.i.*): flow together, stream.

coniunctē (*adv.*): on friendly terms.

coniunctiō, -ōnis (*f.*): connection.

coniunctus, -a, -um: connected, friendly.

coniūrātiō, -ōnis (*f.*): swearing together, conspiracy.

cōnor -ārī, -ātus sum (*v.i.*): try.

conquīrō, -ere, -quīsīvī, -quīsītum (*v.t.*): seek, collect.

cōnscius, -a, -um: sharing knowledge, conscious of, aware of.

cōnscrībō, -ere, -scrīpsī, -scrīptum (*v.t.*): write, compose.

cōnsensiō, -ōnis (*f.*): agreement.

cōnsensus, -ūs (*m.*): agreement.

cōnsentiō, -īre, -sī, -sum (*v.i.*): agree.

cōnsequor, -ī, -secūtus sum (*v.t.* and *i.*): follow, achieve, gain, succeed.

cōnservō, -āre, -āvī, -ātum (*v.t.*): preserve.

cōnsilium -iī (*n.*): plan, advice, resourcefulness.

consōbrīna, -ae (*f.*): cousin.

cōnspiciō, -ere, -spexī, -spectum (*v.t.*): catch sight of.

cōnstantia, -ae (*f.*): firmness.

cōnstituō, -ere, -uī, -ūtum (*v.t.*): draw up, set up, arrange, resolve.

cōnstō, -āre, -stitī (*v.i.*): stand; with *abl.*: consist of; **constat**: it is agreed.

cōnsuescō, -ere, -suēvī, -suētum (*v.i.*): grow accustomed.

cōnsuētūdō, -inis (*f.*): habit, custom, companionship.

cōnsul, -is (*m.*): consul.

cōnsulātus, -ūs (*m.*): consulship.

cōnsulō, -ere, -uī, -sultum (*v.i.* with *dat.*): look after, think of.

cōnsūmō, -ere, -sumpsī, -sumptum (*v.t.*): spend.

contegō, -ere, -texī, -tectum (*v.t.*): cover.

contemnō, -ere, -tempsī, -temptum (*v.t.*): consider of no importance.

contendō, -erc, -dī, -tum (v.i.):
contend, maintain.

contentus, -a, -um: satisfied.

contexō, -ere, -texuī, -textum
(v.t.): weave together.

continēns, -entis: moderate,
restrained.

continentia, -ae (f.): moderation, restraint.

cōntiō, -ōnis (f.): public
assembly.

contrā (adv. and prep. with acc.):
on the other hand, against.

contrārius, -a, -um: opposite;
e contrario: on the other
hand.

conveniō, -īre, -vēnī, -ventum
(v.i. and t.): come together,
meet, fit, agree.

conventus, -ūs (m.): gathering,
assembly.

convertō, -ere, -tī, -sum (v.t.):
turn, change.

convictus, -ūs (m.): living
together, intimate friendship.

convīva, -ae (c.): guest (at a
dinner party).

convīvium, -iī (n.): dinner
party.

cōpiae, -arum (f. pl.): forces.

cōpula, -ae (f.): link.

corōna, -ae (f.): crown.

corpus, -oris (n.): body.

corrumpō, -ere, -rūpī, -rup-
tum (v.t.): corrupt, bribe.

cotīdiānus, -a, -um: daily.

crēdō, -ere, -didī, -ditum
(v.t.): lend, entrust; (with
dat.): believe.

cremō, -āre, -āvī, -ātum (v.t.):
burn (esp. a dead body).

crescō, -ere, crēvī, crētum
(v.i.): grow, increase.

crīmen, -inis (n.): accusation.

crūdēlis, -e: cruel.

crūdēlitās, -ātis (f.): cruelty.

crūdēliter, crūdēlius, crūdēl
issimē (adv.): cruelly.

cubitum, -ī (n.): elbow.

cubō, -āre, cubuī, cubitum
(v.i.): lie down, recline.

culpa, -ae (f.): blame, fault.

cultus, -ūs (m.): culture, elegance, style (esp. of dress).

cum (1) (conj.): when, since,
although; cum . . . tum:
both . . . and; (2) (prep. with
abl.): with.

cupiditās, ātis (f.): desire.

cupiō, -ere, cupīvī, cupītum
(v.t.): desire.

cūra, -ae (f.): care, anxiety,
concern.

cūrātiō, -ōnis (f.): medical
treatment.

cūrō, -āre, -āvī, -ātum (v.t.):
look after, take care of.

custōdia, -ae (f.): guard,
watch.

custōs, -ōdis (c.): guard,
watcher.

D: 500.

damnō, -āre, -āvī, -ātum
(v.t.): condemn.

dē (prep. with abl.): about,
concerning.

dēbeō, -ēre, -uī, -itum (v.t.):
owe, ought.

dēcēdō, -ere, -cessī, -ces-
sum (v.i.): depart, retire, die.

decem: ten.

dēcernō, -ere, -crēvī, -crētum
(v.t.): decide, decree.

decet, -ēre, -uit (impers. with
acc.): it befits, it is fitting.

dēcipiō, -ere, -cēpī, -ceptum
(v.t.): deceive.

dēdō, -ere, dēdidī, dēditum
(v.t.): give up, surrender.

dēdūcō, -ere, -dūxī, -ductum
(v.t.): lead away, induce.

dēferō, -ferre, -tulī, -lātum (*v.t.*): bring, give, offer, report.

dēhortor, -ārī, -ātus sum (*v.t.*): advise not to.

dēiciō, -ere, -iēcī, -iectum (*v.t.*): throw down.

dein, deinde (*adv.*): next, then.

dēlectō, -āre, -āvī, -ātum (*v.t.*): delight.

dēleō, -ēre, -ēvī, -ētum (*v.t.*): destroy, end.

dēlicātē (*adv.*): delicately.

dēlictum, -ī (*n.*): failure, offence.

dēligō, -ere, -lēgī, -lēctum (*v.t.*): choose.

dēmergō, -ere, -sī, -sum (*v.t.*): cause to sink.

dēmigrō, -āre, -āvī, -ātum (*v.i.*): go off.

dēpellō, -ere, -pulī, -pulsum (*v.t.*): drive out, drive away.

dēportō, -āre, -āvī, -ātum (*v.t.*): carry away, bring home.

dēprecor, -ārī, -ātus sum (*v.t.*): pray that something may not happen.

dēprimō, -ere, -pressī, -pressum (*v.t.*): suppress.

dēscendō, -ere, -dī, -sum (*v.i.*): go down.

dēscīscō, -ere, -īvī or **iī, -ītum** (*v.i.*): revolt, desert.

dēscrībō, -ere, -scrīpsī, -scrīptum (*v.t.*): describe.

dēsīderium, -iī (*n.*): longing.

dēsīderō, -āre, -āvī, -ātum (*v.t.*): long for, need.

dēsinō, -ere, -siī, -situm (*v.t.*): cease.

dēsistō, -ere, -stitī, -stitum (*v.i.*): cease.

dēspērō, -āre, -āvī, -ātum (*v.i.* and *t.*): despair, despair of; **dēspērātus, -a, -um**: desperate.

dēspiciō, -ere, -spexī, -spectum (*v.t.*): despise.

dēspondeō, -ēre, -spondī, -spōnsum (*v.t.*): promise, betroth.

dēstituō, -ere, -uī, -ūtum (*v.t.*): desert, abandon.

dēsum, -esse, -fuī (*v.i.*): be lacking, fail.

dētegō, -ere, -texī, -tectum (*v.t.*): uncover.

dēterreō, -ēre, -uī, -itum (*v.t.*): frighten off, deter.

dētrīmentum, -ī (*n.*): loss.

dēvehō, -ere, -vexī, -vectum (*v.t.*): take away.

dēvinciō, -īre, -vinxī, -vinctum (*v.t.*): bind down.

dēvōtiō, -ōnis (*f.*): cursing.

dēvoveō, -ēre, -vōvī, -vōtum (*v.t.*): curse.

dicis (*gen. sing.*): judicial form (used only in phrase **dicis causā** or **gratiā**).

dīcō, -ere, dīxī, dictum (*v.t.*): say, speak.

dictitō, -ere, -āvī, -ātum (*v.t.*): keep on saying.

dictum, -ī (*n.*): word, remark.

diēs, -ēī (*m.*): day; **in dies**: daily.

differō, -ferre, distulī, dīlātum (*v.t.*): spread abroad.

difficilis, -e: difficult.

diffīdō, -ere, -fīsus sum (*v.i.* with *dat.*): distrust.

dīgnitās, -ātis (*f.*): dignity, worth, rank.

dīgnus, -a, -um: worthy; (with *abl.*): worthy of.

dīligēns, -entis: careful, thrifty.

dīligenter (*adv.*): carefully.

dīligentia, -ae (*f.*): care, diligence.

dīligō, -ere, -lēxī, -lēctum (*v.t.*): like, love.

dīmicō, -āre, -āvī, -ātum (*v.i.*): fight.

dīmittō, -ere, -mīsī, -missum (*v.t.*): send away, throw away.

dīs, dītior, dītissimus: rich.

discēdō, -ere, -cessī, -cessum (*v.i.*): depart.

disertus, -a, -um: eloquent.

disiciō, -ere, -iēcī, -iectum (*v.t.*): throw apart, break up.

dispertiō, -īre, -īvī, -ītum (*v.t.*): distribute.

displiceō, -ēre, -uī, -itum (*v.i.* with *dat.*): displease.

dissensiō, -ōnis (*f.*): disagreement.

dissideō, -ēre, -sēdī, -sessum (*v.i.*): disagree, oppose.

dissimilitūdō, -inis (*f.*): unlikeness, difference.

dissociō, -āre, -āvī, -ātum (*v.t.*): divide.

dissolūtus, -a, -um: dissolute.

distineō, -ēre, -uī, -tentum (*v.t.*): hold apart, distract.

diū, diūtius, diūtissimē (*adv.*): for a long time.

diūtinus, -a, -um: lasting a long time.

dīversus, -a, -um: different.

dīves, -itis: rich.

dīvīdō, -ere, -sī, -sum (*v.t.*): divide.

dīvīnātiō, -ōnis (*f.*): divination, prophecy.

dīvīnus, -a, -um: divine.

dīvitiae, -ārum (*f. pl.*): riches, wealth.

dīvus, -a, -um: divine, deified.

dō, dare, dedī, datum (*v.t.*): give.

doceō, -ēre, docuī, doctum (*v.t.*): teach, inform.

docilis, -e: teachable, quick to learn.

docilitās, -ātis (*f.*): teachability, quickness in learning.

doctrīna, -ae (*f.*): teaching, learning, principle.

dōdrāns, -antis (*m.*): nine-twelfths of anything; **hēres ex dōdrante**: heir to three-quarters of the property.

dolor, -ōris (*m.*): grief, pain.

domesticus, -a, -um: of a house, domestic, private.

domicilium, -iī (*n.*): dwelling, abode.

domus, -ūs (*f.*): house, home.

dōnō, -āre, -āvī, -ātum (*v.t.*): present, give.

dubitō, -āre, -āvī, -ātum (*v.t.*): doubt.

ducentī, -ae, -a: 200.

dūcō, -ere, dūxī, ductum (*v.t.*): lead, consider, prolong.

dulcis, -e: sweet.

duo, -ae, -o: two.

dūritia, -ae (*f.*): hardness.

dux, ducis (*m.*): leader, general.

ē (*prep.* with *abl.*): from, in accordance with; **ē rēpūblicā**: in the interests of the State.

ēditus, -a, -um: high.

ēdō, -ere, -didī, -ditum (*v.t.*): give out, publish.

ēdūcō, -āre, -āvī, -ātum (*v.t.*): bring up.

efferō, -ferre, extulī, ēlātum (*v.t.*): carry away (esp. for burial), raise up, spread abroad; **ēlātus**: puffed up.

efficiō, -ere, -fēcī, -fectum (*v.t.*): achieve, bring about.

**effringō, -ere, -frēgī, -frac-
tum** (*v.t.*): break open.

effugiō, -ere, -fūgī, -fugitum
(*v.i.*): escape.

effūsus, -a, -um: profuse,
lavish.

ego: I; **egomet:** I myself.

ēgredior, -ī, -gressus sum
(*v.i.*): come out.

ēiciō, -ere, -iēcī, -iectum (*v.t.*):
throw out.

ēlegāns, -antis: elegant, fine.

ēlegantia, -ae (*f.*): elegance,
refinement.

ēliciō, -ere, -uī, -itum (*v.t.*):
entice out.

ēligō, -ere, -lēgī, -lectum
(*v.t.*): select.

ēloquentia, -ae (*f.*): eloquence.

emax, -ācis: fond of buying.

ēmergō, -ere, -sī, -sum (*v.t.*):
raise up.

ēminus (*adv.*): at long range.

emō, -ere, ēmī, emptum
(*v.t.*): buy.

enim (*conj.*): for.

ēnumerō, -āre, -āvī, -ātum
(*v.t.*): enumerate, list.

eō (*adv.*): to that place, thither.

eō, īre, īvī and iī, itum (*v.i.*):
go.

eōdem (*adv.*): to the same place.

ephēmeris, -idis (*f.*): diary,
account book.

epistula, -ae (*f.*): letter.

epulum, -ī (*n.*), **epulae, -arum**
(*f. pl.*): banquet.

eques, -itis (*m.*): horseman,
knight.

equester, -tris, -tre: belonging to a knight.

ergā (*prep.* with *acc.*): towards
(of emotions).

ergō (*adv.*): therefore.

ēripiō, -ere, -ripuī, -reptum
(*v.t.*): snatch away.

ērudiō, -īre, -īvī and -iī, -itum
(*v.t.*): educate, teach.

ērumpō, -ere, -rūpī, -ruptum
(*v.i.*): break out.

et (*conj.*): and; **et . . . et:**
both . . . and.

etiam (*conj.*): also, even.

etsī (*conj.*): even if.

ēvādō, -ere, -sī, -sum (*v.i.*):
go out, result.

ēveniō, -īre, -vēnī, -ventum
(*v.i.*): happen.

ēvītō, -āre, -āvī, -ātum (*v.t.*):
avoid.

ex (*prep.* with *abl.*): from, in
accordance with.

exaudiō, -īre, -īvī, -ītum (*v.t.*):
hear clearly.

excellenter (*adv.*): excellently.

excellō, -ere, -uī (*v.i.*): be
outstanding.

excipiō, -ere, -cēpī, -ceptum
(*v.t.*): take upon oneself.

excitō, -āre, -āvī, -ātum (*v.t.*):
rouse.

excōgitō, -āre, -āvī, -ātum
(*v.t.*): think out, devise.

exemplum, -ī (*n.*): example,
copy.

exeō, -īre, -iī, -itum (*v.i.*): go
out, set out.

exerceō, -ēre, -uī, -itum (*v.t.*):
exercise.

exercitus, -ūs (*m.*): army,
troops.

exhauriō, -īre, -sī, -stum
(*v.t.*): drain, exhaust.

eximō, -ere, -ēmī, -emptum
(*v.t.*): take out, remove.

existimātiō, -ōnis (*f.*): reputation.

existimō, -āre, -āvī, -ātum
(*v.t.*): think, consider.

**expediō, -īre, -īvī and -iī,
-ītum** (*v.t.*): extricate, re-
lease.

expellō, -ēre, -pulī, -pulsum
(*v.t.*): drive out.

expendō, -ere, -dī, -sum (*v.t.*):
pay out.

experior, -īrī, -pertus sum
(*v.t.*): try, experiment.

expers, -pertis (with *gen.*):
without a share in.

**expōnō, -ere, -posuī, -posi-
tum** (*v.t.*): set forth, explain.

expugnō, -āre, -āvī, -ātum
(*v.t.*): take by storm.

expulsor, -ōris (*m.*): expeller.

exsilium, -iī (*n.*): exile.

exsistō, -ere, -stitī, -stitum
(*v.i.*): arise, occur.

exspectātiō, -ōnis (*f.*): eagerness.

exspectō, -āre, -āvī, -ātum
(*v.t.*): await.

exsplendescō, -ere, -splenduī
(*v.i.*): begin to shine out.

exstinguō, -ere, -nxī, -nctum
(*v.t.*): extinguish.

extollō, -ere (*v.t.*): raise up,
extol.

extrēmus, -a, -um: latest, last.

faber, -brī (*m.*): craftsman,
army mechanic.

facile, -lius, -llimē (*adv.*):
easily.

facilis, -e: easy.

facilitās, -ātis (*f.*): friendli-
ness.

facinus, -oris (*n.*): deed,
crime.

faciō, -ere, fēcī, factum (*v.t.*):
make, do, perform.

factiō, -ōnis (*f.*): political
party, supporters.

factum, -ī (*n.*): deed.

facultās, -ātis (*f.*): opportunity; *pl.*: property.

faenus, -oris (*n.*): interest.

fallō, -ere, fefellī, falsum
(*v.t.*): deceive.

falsō (*adv.*): falsely.

falsus, -a, -um: false.

fāma, -ae (*f.*): reputation,
report.

familia, -as and **-ae** (*f.*):
family.

familiāris, -is (*m.*): friend;
(*adj.*): of the family.

familiāritās, -ātis (*f.*): familiarity, friendship.

familiāriter (*adv.*): familiarly.

fastīgium, -iī (*n.*): height,
summit, position.

fateor, -ērī, fassus sum (*v.t.*):
admit.

fautor, -ōris (*m.*): favourer,
supporter.

faveō, -ēre, fāvī, fautum (*v.i.*
with *dat.*): favour, support.

febris, -is (*f.*): fever.

fenestra, -ae (*f.*): window.

ferō, ferre, tulī, lātum (*v.t.*):
bear, carry, win, produce,
report, extol.

ferrum, -ī (*n.*): iron, sword.

ferus, -a, -um: fierce.

festus, -a, -um: festal, holy.

fidēliter (*adv.*): faithfully.

fidēs, -ēī (*f.*): faith, loyalty.

fīlia, -ae (*f.*): daughter.

fīlius, -iī and **-ī** (*m.*): son.

fingō, -ere, finxī, fictum (*v.t.*):
fashion, invent.

fīnis, -is (*m.*): end.

fīō, fierī, factus sum (*v.i.*):
become, happen, be made.

firmitās, -ātis (*f.*): firmness,
strength.

fistula, -ae (*f.*): pipe, ulcer.

flagitō, -āre, -āvī, -ātum (*v.t.*):
demand.

flagrō, -āre, -āvī, -ātum (*v.i.*):
burn.

flamma, -ae (*f.*): flame.

fleō, -ēre, -ēvī, -ētum (*v.i.* and *t.*): weep, weep for.

flōreō, -ēre, -uī (*v.i.*): flower, flourish, prosper.

fluctus, -ūs (*m.*): wave.

flūmen, -minis (*n.*): river.

forensis, -e: of the forum.

foris, -is (*f.*): door, gate.

foris (*adv.*): outside, from outside.

forma, -ae (*f.*): appearance.

formōsus, -a, -um: good-looking.

forte (*abl.* of **fors**, used as *adv.*): by chance.

fortiter, -tius, -tissimē (*adv.*): bravely.

fortūna, -ae (*f.*): chance, fortune.

frangō, -ere, frēgī, fractum (*v.t.*): break.

frāter, -tris (*m.*): brother.

fraus, -dis (*f.*): trickery, deception.

frequēns, -entis: frequent.

frequentia, -ae (*f.*): crowd.

frētus, -a, -um (with *abl.*): relying on.

fructus, -ūs (*m.*): fruit, profit.

frūmentum, -ī (*n.*): corn.

fruor, -ī, fructus sum (*v.i.* with *abl.*): enjoy.

frustrā (*adv.*): in vain.

fuga, -ae (*f.*): flight, exile.

fugiō, -ere, fūgī, fugitum (*v.i.* and *t.*): flee, escape the notice of.

fundus, -ī (*m.*): farm, country estate.

fūnus, -eris (*n.*): funeral.

futūrus, -a, -um: future.

gener, -erī (*m.*): son-in-law.

generō, -āre, -āvī, -ātum (*v.t.*): produce.

generōsus, -a, -um: noble, distinguished, nobly-born.

gēns, -ntis (*f.*): race, nation.

genus, -eris (*n.*): family, kind.

gerō, -ere, gessī, gestum (*v.t.*): carry on, do, hold; **se gerere**: conduct oneself, act.

gladius, -iī (*m.*): sword.

globus, -ī (*m.*): ball, group.

glōrior, -ārī, -ātus sum (*v.i.*): boast, pride oneself.

glōriōsus, -a, -um: glorious.

Graecē (*adv.*): in Greek.

grātia, -ae (*f.*): grace, favour, influence; **grātiā** with *gen.*: for the sake of.

grātus, -a, -um: pleasing, grateful.

gravis, -e: heavy, serious, important.

gravitās, -ātis (*f.*): seriousness

gubernātor, -ōris (*m.*): helmsman.

habeō, -ēre, -uī, -itum (*v.t.*): have, hold, consider.

habitō, -āre, -āvī, -ātum (*v.i.*): dwell, live.

hāctenus (*adv.*): so far, this far.

hasta, -ae (*f.*): spear; **hasta publica**: public auction.

hērēditās, -ātis (*f.*): inheritance.

hērēs, -ēdis (*c.*): heir.

hīc (*adv.*): here.

hīc, haec, hōc: this.

hiems, hiemis (*f.*): winter, storm.

historia, -ae (*f.*): history.

historicus, -ī (*m.*): historian.

homō, -minis (*m.*): man.

honōs, -ōris (*m.*): honour, office.

hortor, -ārī, -ātus sum (*v.t.*): urge.

hortus, -ī (*m.*): garden.
hospes, -itis (*m.*): host, guest.
hostis, -is (*m.*): enemy.
HS: symbol for **sestertius** (*v.* note Att. IV. 3).
hūc (*adv.*): hither, to this place.
hūmānitās, -ātis (*f.*): civilisation, culture, refinement.
humilis, -e: humble.

iactō, -āre, -āvī, -ātum (*v.t.*): toss.
iam (*adv.*): now, already.
iānua, -ae (*f.*): door.
ibi (*adv.*): there.
īdem, eadem, idem: same; **īdem atque**: the same as.
ideō (*adv.*) : therefore.
idōneus, -a, -um: suitable.
igitur (*conj.*): therefore.
ignis, -is (*m.*): fire.
ignōrō, -āre, -āvī, -ātum (*v.t.*): be unaware of.
ille, -a, -ud: that, he, she, it, etc.
illūc (*adv.*): thither, to that place.
illustris, -e: distinguished, famous.
imāgō, -inis (*f.*): likeness, bust.
imbuō, -ere, -buī, -būtum (*v.t.*): stain, infect.
imitātor, -ōris (*m.*): imitator.
imitor, -ārī, -ātus sum (*v.t.*): imitate.
immerēns, -entis: undeserving.
immoderātus, -a, -um: unrestrained, excessive.
immodestia, -ae (*f.*): lack of discipline.
immortālis, -e: undying.
impediō, -īre, -īvī, -ītum (*v.t.*): hinder.
impendeō, -ēre (*v.i.*): overhang, be imminent, threaten.

imperātor, -ōris (*m.*): commander, emperor.
imperium, -iī (*n.*): power, authority, command, government.
imperō, -āre, -āvī, -ātum (*v.t. and i. with dat.*): demand, command.
impertiō, -īre, -īvī and -iī, -ītum (*v.t.*): impart.
impetus, -ūs (*m.*): attack.
implicō, -āre, -āvī and -uī, -ātum and -itum (*v.t.*): entangle, involve.
impōnō, -ere, -posuī, -positum (*v.t.*): place on.
imprīmīs (*adv.*): especially.
imprūdentia, -ae (*f.*): lack of caution.
īmus, -a, -um: lowest.
in (*prep. with acc.*): to, towards, into; (*with abl.*): in.
inānis, -e: empty.
incendium, -iī (*n.*): fire.
incidō, -ere, -cidī, -cāsum (*v.i.*): fall into, happen, occur.
incīdō, -ere, -cīdī, -cīsum (*v.t.*): cut in, inscribe.
incitō, -āre, -āvī, -ātum (*v.t.*): stimulate.
incolumitās, -ātis (*f.*): safety.
incommodum, -ī (*n.*): misfortune.
incūria, -ae (*f.*): neglect.
inde (*adv.*): from there, thence, then.
indicium, -iī (*n.*): sign, proof.
indicō, -āre, -āvī, -ātum (*v.t.*): indicate, reveal.
indīcō, -ēre, -dīxī, -dictum (*v.t.*): declare (esp. war).
indigeō, -ēre, -uī (*v.i. with abl.*): be in need of.
indignor, -ārī, -ātus sum (*v.t.*): consider unworthy, be indignant at.

indiligēns, -entis: negligent.
indūcō, -ere, -dūxī, -ductum (*v.t.*): bring in.
indulgentia, -ae (*f.*): indulgence, fondness.
indulgeō, -ēre, -sī, -tum (*v.i.* with *dat.*): indulge, give way to.
industria, -ae (*f*): industry.
ineō, -īre, -iī, -itum (*v.t.*): enter, begin.
inermis, -e: unarmed.
inertia, -ae (*f.*): idleness.
infāmia, -ae (*f.*): disrepute.
infāmō, -āre, -āvī, -ātum (*v.t.*): speak ill of.
infimus, -a, -um: lowest.
infīnītus, -a, -um: endless.
ingenium, -iī (*n.*): intellect, ability, talent.
iniciō, -ere, -iēcī, -iectum (*v.t.*): throw into, inspire.
inimīcitia, -ae (*f.*): personal enmity.
inimīcus, -ī (*m.*): personal enemy.
initium, -iī (*n.*): beginning.
iniūria, -ae (*f.*): wrong.
innītor, -ī, -nixus and -nīsus sum (*v.i.*): lean upon.
inopia, -ae (*f.*): want, lack of resource.
inopinātus, -a, -um: unexpected.
inquam (*def. vb.*): say; **inquit:** he says, he said.
inscius, -a, -um: ignorant.
insequor, -ī, -secūtus sum (*v.t.*): pursue, attack.
inserviō, -īre, -īvī and -iī, -itum (*v.i.* with *dat.*): serve, respect.
insiliae, -ārum (*f. pl.*): ambush, trap, plot.
instituō, -ere, -uī, -ūtum (*v.t.*): set up, begin, determine.

institūtum, -ī (*n.*): practice, mode of life.
instō, -āre, -stitī (*v.i.*): press on.
insuētus, -a, -um: unaccustomed.
insula, -ae (*f.*): island.
intellegō, -ere, -lēxī, -lēctum (*v.t.*): realise, understand, distinguish.
intemperāns, -antis: lacking self-control, immoderate.
intemperanter (*adv.*): immoderately.
inter (*prep.* with *acc.*): among, between; **inter se timere:** to fear one another.
intercēdō, -ere, -cessī, -cessum (*v.i.*): come between, intervene, interfere.
interdum (*adv.*): sometimes.
intereō, -īre, -iī, -itum (*v.i.*): perish.
interfector, -ōris (*m.*): killer.
interficiō, -ere, -fēcī, -fectum (*v.t.*): kill.
interim (*adv.*): meanwhile.
interimō, -ere, -ēmī, -emptum (*v.t.*): destroy.
interitus, -ūs (*m.*): ruin, death.
interpōnō, -ere, -posuī, -positum (*v.t.*): interpose.
interpretor, -ārī, -ātus sum (*v.t.*): explain.
intersum, -esse, -fuī (*v.i.* with *dat.*): be among, be present at.
intestīnum, -ī (*n.*): intestine.
intimē (*adv.*): intimately.
intimus, -a, -um: inmost, intimate.
intrō, -āre, -āvī, -ātum (*v.i.* and *t.*): enter.
introeō, -īre, -iī, -itum (*v.i.*): enter.
intrōmittō, -ere, -mīsī, -missum (*v.t.*): admit.

intueor, -ērī, -tuitus sum (*v.t.*): look at, bear in mind.

invādō, -ere, -vāsī, -vāsum (*v.i.* and *t.*): attack.

inveniō, -īre, -vēnī, -ventum (*v.t.*): come upon, find.

inveterāsco, -ere, -rāvī (*v.i.*): grow old, become established.

invidia, -ae (*f.*): malice, ill-feeling, disfavour.

invīsus, -a, -um: hated.

invītō, -āre, -āvī, -ātum (*v.t.*): invite.

invītus, -a, -um: unwilling.

iocor, -ārī, -ātus sum (*v.i.*): joke.

ipse, -a, -um: -self.

īra, -ae (*f.*): anger.

īrascor, -ī, īrātus sum (*v.i.* with *dat.*): become angry.

is, ea, id: he, she, it, etc.; this, that.

ita (*adv.*): so, thus.

itaque (*conj.*): and so, accordingly.

iter, itineris (*n.*): journey.

iubeō, -ēre, iussī, iussum (*v.t.*): order, bid.

iūcundus, -a, -um: pleasing, delightful.

iūdicium, -iī (*n.*): judgment, legal decision.

iūdicō, -āre, -āvī, -ātum (*v.t.*): judge.

iūrō, -āre, -āvī, -ātum (*v.i.*): swear.

iūs, iūris (*n.*): right, justice, law.

iuvō, -āre, iūvī, iūtum (*v.t.*): help.

iuxtā (*adv.* and *prep.* with *acc.*): near.

Kalendae, -arum (*f. pl.*): Kalends, first day of the month.

L: Lūcius (Roman *praenomen*); 50.

labor, -ōris (*m.*): toil, hard work.

labōriōsus, -a, -um: hard-working, involving hard work.

lacrima, -ae (*f.*): tear.

lacrumō, -āre, -āvī, -ātum (*v.i.* and *t.*): weep, weep for.

laedō, -ere, -sī, -sum (*v.t.*): harm.

laetitia, -ae (*f.*): joy.

lapideus, -a, -um: of stone.

lapis, -idis (*m.*): stone, milestone.

largitiō, -ōnis (*f.*): distribution, liberality.

lateō, -ēre, -uī (*v.i.*): lie hidden.

Latīnē (*adv.*): in Latin.

laudō, -āre, -āvī, -ātum (*v.t.*): praise.

laus, -dis (*f.*): praise.

lautus, -a, -um: washed, cultured, distinguished.

lēcticula, -ae (*f.*): small litter, bier.

lēctiō, -ōnis (*f.*): reading.

lēctor, -ōris (*m.*): reader.

lēctus, -ī (*m.*): bed, couch.

legātiō, -ōnis (*f.*): embassy, duty delegated to another, staff appointment.

legātus, -ī (*m.*): representative, deputy governor.

legō, -ere, lēgī, lēctum (*v.t.*): read.

lēniō, -īre, -īvī and -iī, -ītum (*v.t.*): soften.

lepōs, -ōris (*m.*): grace, charm.

levis, -e: light, trivial irresponsible.

levō, -āre, -āvī, -ātum (*v.t.*): lighten, relieve.

lēx, lēgis (*f.*): law.

I

liber, -brī (*m.*): book.
līberālis, -e: generous.
līberālitās, -ātis (*f.*): generosity.
līberāliter (*adv.*): generously.
līberātor, -ōris (*m.*): liberator.
līberē (*adv.*): freely.
līberī, -ōrum (*m. pl.*): children.
līberō, -āre, -āvī, -ātum (*v.t.*): set free.
lībertās, -ātis (*f.*): liberty.
libīdinōsus, -a, -um: sensual, licentious.
librārius, -iī (*m.*): copyist, scribe.
licenter (*adv.*): without restraint.
licentia, -ae (*f.*): lack of restraint.
licitus, -a, -um: permitted.
lignum, -ī (*n.*): firewood.
līmen, -minis (*n.*): threshold, doorway.
lingua, -ae (*f.*): tongue, language.
līs, lītis (*f.*): lawsuit.
litterae, -ārum (*f. pl.*): letter, literature.
litterātus, -a, -um: learned, educated.
locuplētō, -āre, -āvī, -ātum (*v.t.*): enrich.
locus, -ī (*m.*) *pl.* **loca, -ōrum** (*n.*): place, position.
longē, -ius, -issimē (*adv.*): far; **nōn longius:** no longer.
longus, -a, -um: long; **navis longa:** warship.
loquor, -ī, locūtus sum (*v.t. and i.*): speak, say.
lūdus, -ī (*m.*): school.
lumbus, -ī (*m.*): loin.
lūxuria, -ae (*f.*): luxury, extravagance.
lūxuriōse (*adv.*): luxuriously, extravagantly.

lūxuriōsus, -a, -um: luxurious, extravagant.

M: Marcus (Roman *praenomen*); 1000.
magis (*compar. adv.*): more.
magistrātus, -ūs (*m.*): magistrate, magistracy.
māgnificus, -a, -um: pretentious.
māgnitūdō, -inis (*f.*): size, greatness.
māgnus, -a, -um: great.
māior, -ius (*compar. adj.*): greater; **maiores:** ancestors.
male (*adv.*): badly; **rem male gerere:** be unsuccessful.
maledicus, -a, -um: speaking evil, abusive.
malitiōsē (*adv.*): treacherously.
mālō, mālle, māluī (*v.t.*): prefer.
malus, -a, -um: bad, evil.
manceps, -cipis (*m.*): purchaser, contractor, tax-farmer.
mandō, -āre, -āvī, -ātum (*v.t.*): entrust, commit to another's care.
maneō, -ēre, mānsī, mānsum (*v.i.*): remain.
manus, -ūs (*f.*): hand, band.
mare, -is (*n.*): sea.
maritimus, -a, -um: of the sea.
māter, -tris (*f.*): mother.
mātrimōnium, -iī (*n.*): marriage.
mātūrē (*adv.*): early.
mātūrō, -āre, -āvī, -ātum (*v.i. and t.*): hurry.
mātūrus, -a, -um: early.
māximē (*sup. adv.*): very greatly, most.
māximus, -a, -um (*sup. adj.*): greatest.

medicīna, -ae (*f.*): medicine, medical skill.

medicus, -ī (*m.*): doctor.

medimnus, -ī (*m.*): medimnus (Greek measure of corn), a bushel.

mediōcris, -e: moderate, average.

meminī, -isse (*def. vb.*): remember.

memor, -oris (with *gen.*): mindful.

memoria, -ae (*f.*): memory.

mendācium, -iī (*n.*): lie.

mēns, mentis (*f.*): mind.

mēnsis, -is (*m.*): month.

mēnsūra, -ae (*f.*): measure, measurement.

mentiō, -ōnis (*f.*): mention.

meritō (*adv.*): deservedly.

mētior, -īrī, mēnsus sum (*v.t.*): measure.

metuō, -ere, metuī, metūtum (*v.t.*): fear.

meus, -a, -um: my.

migrō, -āre, -āvī, -ātum (*v.i.*): go away.

mīles, -itis (*m.*): soldier.

mīlle, *pl.* **mīlia:** 1000.

minuō, -ere, -uī, -ūtum (*v.t.*): lessen.

minus (*compar. adv.*): less.

mīrābiliter (*adv.*): remarkably.

misericordia, -ae (*f.*): pity.

miseror, -ārī, -ātus sum (*v.i. and t.*): pity, feel pity.

mittō, -ere, mīsī, missum (*v.t.*): send.

mōbilitās, -ātis (*f.*): fickleness, changeableness.

moderātiō, -ōnis (*f.*): moderation.

modicus, -a, -um: moderate, modest.

modius, -iī (*m.*): peck, sixth part of Greek bushel.

modo (*adv.*): merely, only; **modo . . . modo:** now . . . now.

modus, -ī (*m.*): way, manner, kind.

mōlestus, -a, -um: burdensome, troublesome.

mōlior, -īrī, -ītus sum (*v.t.*): attempt (something difficult).

mōmentum -ī (*n.*): importance.

moneō, -ēre, -uī, -itum (*v.t.*): warn.

monumentum, -ī (*n.*): memorial.

morbus, -ī (*m.*): illness.

morior, -ī, mortuus sum (*v.i.*): die.

moror, -ārī, -ātus sum (*v.t. and i.*): delay, stay.

mors, mortis (*f.*): death.

mōs, mōris (*m.*): custom, way; (*pl.*): character; **morem gerere** with *dat.*: allow to have own way.

moveō, -ēre, mōvī, mōtum (*v.t.*): move.

muliebris, -e: of a woman.

mulier, -eris (*f.*): woman.

multiplicō, -āre, -āvī, -ātum (*v.t.*): multiply, increase.

multitūdō, -inis (*f.*): multitude, common people.

multus, -a, -um: much, many; **multō** (*abl. neut.* used as *adv.*): much, by much.

munditia, -ae (*f.*): cleanliness, elegance.

mūniō, -īre, -īvī and -iī, -ītum (*v.t.*): fortify.

mūnus, -eris (*n.*): gift.

mūtātiō, -ōnis (*f.*): change.

mūtō, -āre, -āvī, -ātum (*v.t.*): change.

mystērium, -iī (*n.*): mystery, secret ceremony.

nam (*conj.*): for.
namque (*conj.*): for indeed.
nancīscor, -ī, nactus sum (*v.t.*): obtain, meet with.
nāscor, -ī, nātus sum (*v.i.*): be born.
nātīvus, -a, -um: inborn, innate.
nātūra, -ae (*f.*): nature.
nātūrālis, -e: natural.
nauticus, -a, -um: naval.
nāvālis, -e: naval.
nāvis, -is (*f.*): ship.
nē (*conj.*): lest, so that . . . not; **nē . . . quidem** (*adv.*): not even.
nec: see **neque**.
necessāriō (*adv.*): of necessity.
necessārius, -a, -um: necessary.
necesse (*indecl. adj.*): necessary.
necessitūdō, -inis (*f.*): close relationship, friendship.
nefās (*indecl. n.*): wrong, a crime against the gods.
neglegenter (*adv.*): negligently.
negō, -āre, -āvī, -ātum (*v.t.*): deny, refuse.
negōtium, -iī (*n.*): business, task, trouble.
nēmō (*irreg.*): nobody, no one.
neptis, -is (*f.*): granddaughter.
neque or **nec** (*conj.*): nor, and not; **neque . . . neque**: neither . . . nor.
nesciō, -ire, -īvī and **-iī, -ītum** (*v.t.*): not know, be ignorant.
nesciōquis, -quid: someone, something, I don't know who (what).
neuter, -tra, -trum: neither.
nihil (*indecl. n.*): nothing; **nihilō sētius**: nevertheless.
nimis (*adv.*): too much, excessively.
nimius, -a, -um: excessive.

nisi (*conj.*): if not, unless.
nītor, -ī, nīsus or **nīxus sum** (*v.i.*): strive.
nōbilis, -e: nobly born, noble.
noceō, -ēre, -uī, -itum (*v.i.* with *dat.*): harm.
noctū (*adv.*): by night.
nōlō, nōlle, nōluī (*v.i.*): be unwilling, refuse.
nōmen, -inis (*n.*): name, reputation.
nōn (*adv.*): not.
nōnāgintā: ninety.
nōnnullī, -ae, -a: not none, i.e. several.
nōtitia, -ae (*f.*): being known, knowledge.
notō, -āre, -āvī, -ātum (*v.t.*): mark, indicate.
nōs: we.
noster, -tra, -trum: our.
novus, -a, -um: new.
nox, noctis (*f.*): night.
noxius, -a, -um: guilty.
nūbō, -ere, nūpsī, nuptum (*v.i.* with *dat.*): marry (of the wife).
nūllus, -a, -um: no.
numerus, -ī (*m.*): number.
numquam (*adv.*): never.
nunc (*adv.*): now.
nūntius, -iī (*m.*): messenger, message.
nuptiae, -arum (*f. pl.*): marriage.
nusquam (*adv.*): nowhere.

ob (*prep.* with *acc.*): on account of.
obeō, -īre, -iī, -itum (*v.t.*): meet, undertake.
oblīvīscor, -ī, -lītus sum (*v.t.* and *i.*): forget.
obruō, -ere, -ruī, -rutum (*v.t.*): overwhelm, surfeit.

obsecrō, -āre, -āvī, -ātum
(*v.t.*): beseech.

obsequium, -iī (*n.*): following,
compliance, giving way.

obsequor, -ī, -secūtus sum
(*v.i.* with *dat.*): follow, attend
to.

obserō, -āre, -āvī, -ātum
(*v.t.*): bolt.

observantia, -ae (*f.*): courtesy.

obsidiō, -ōnis (*f.*): siege.

obstinātiō, -ōnis (*f.*): determination.

obstō, -āre, -stitī (*v.i.* with
dat.): stand in the way,
thwart.

obsum, -esse, -fuī (*v.i.* with
dat.): be a hindrance.

obtineō, -ēre, -tinuī, -tentum
(*v.t.*): hold, occupy.

obtrectātiō, -ōnis (*f.*): disparagement.

obviam (*adv.*): in the way, to
meet.

occāsiō, -ōnis (*f.*): opportunity.

occīdō, -ere, -cīdī, -cīsum
(*v.t.*): kill.

occulō, -ere, -uī, -cultum
(*v t*): hide, conceal

occupātiō, -ōnis (*f*): pre-
occupation.

occupō, -āre, -āvī, -ātum
(*v.t.*): occupy, preoccupy.

oculus, -ī (*m.*): eye.

ōdī, -isse (*def. vb.*): hate.

odiōsus, -a, -um: hateful.

odium, -iī (*n.*): hatred.

offendō, -ere, -dī, -fēnsum
(*v.t.*): offend, displease.

offēnsiō, -ōnis (*f.*): offence,
quarrel.

officium, -iī (*n.*): service, duty.

omnis, -e: all, every.

onerārius, -a, -um: freight-
carrying.

onustus, -a, -um: laden.

opera, -ae (*f.*): work, attention; **operam dare**: take
trouble.

opīniō, -ōnis (*f.*): belief,
opinion.

opīnor, -ārī, -ātus sum (*v.i.*):
believe, suppose.

opperior, -īrī, oppertus and
opperītus sum (*v.i.* and *t.*):
wait, wait for.

oppidum, -ī (*n.*): town.

**opprimō, -ere, -pressī, -pres-
sum** (*v.t.*): crush, suppress.

oppugnō, -āre, -āvī, -ātum
(*v.t.*): attack.

(ops), opis (*f.*): help; (*pl.*):
resources, power.

optimātēs, -um and **-ium**
(*c. pl.*): 'best' men, upper class.

optimus, -a, -um (*sup. adj.*):
best, excellent.

opus, -eris (*n.*): work; **opus
est**: there is need of.

ōra, -ae (*f.*): coast.

ōrātiō, -ōnis (*f.*): speech.

orbis, -is (*m.*): circle; **orbis
terrarum**: the world.

ordinō, -āre, -āvī, -ātum (*v.t.*):
set in order.

ordior, -īrī, orsus sum (*v.t.*):
begin.

ordō, -inis (*m.*): order, class.

orīgō, -inis (*f.*): origin.

orior, -īrī, ortus sum (*v.i.*):
arise, spring, descend from.

ornāmentum -ī (*n.*): adorn-
ment, honour.

ornō, -āre, -āvī, -ātum (*v.t.*):
equip, adorn.

ōrō, -āre, -āvī, -ātum (*v.t.*):
beg.

ōs, ōris (*n.*): mouth, face.

ōsculor, -ārī, -ātus sum (*v.t.*):
kiss.

ostendō, -ere, -dī, -sum and **-tum** (*v.t.*): show.

ostentātiō, -ōnis (*f.*): outward show.

P: Publius (Roman *praenomen*).

pactiō, -ōnis (*f.*): agreement, terms.

paene (*adv.*): almost, nearly.

palam (*adv.*): openly; **palam facio:** make known.

pār, paris: equal, right, fair, like; **pari modo:** likewise.

parēns, -entis (*c.*): parent.

pāreō, -ēre, -uī, -itum (*v.i.* with *dat.*): obey.

pario, -ere, peperī, partum (*v.t.*): produce.

parō, -āre, -āvī, -ātum (*v.t.*): prepare, procure.

pars, partis (*f.*): part, share, party.

parsimōnia, -ae (*f.*): frugality.

partim (*adv.*): partly.

partior, -īrī, -ītus sum (*v.t.*): divide.

parum (*adv.*): too little, insufficiently.

pateō, -ēre, -uī (*v.t.*): lie open.

pater, -tris (*m.*): father.

patiēns, -entis: patient.

patientia, -ae (*f.*): patience, endurance.

patior, -ī, passus sum (*v.t.*): suffer, allow.

patria, -ae (*f.*): native land.

patrimōnium, -iī (*n.*): patrimony, inheritance.

paucus, -a, -um: few.

paulō (*adv.*): a little.

pāx, pācis (*f.*): peace.

pecūnia, -ae (*f.*): money.

pecūniōsus, -a, -um: wealthy.

pedes, -itis (*m.*): footsoldier.

pedester, -tris, -tre: on foot.

pedisequus, -ī (*m.*): footman, page.

penes (*prep.* with *acc.*): in the power of.

penitus (*adv.*): deeply, fully.

per (*prep.* with *acc.*): through.

peraeque (*adv.*): evenly, on an average.

peragō, -ere, -ēgī, -actum (*v.t.*): carry out.

percellō, -ere, -culī, -culsum (*v.t.*): strike, overthrow, ruin.

percipiō, -ere, -cēpī, -ceptum (*v.t.*): receive, grasp, understand.

perditus, -a, -um: abandoned, depraved.

perdūcō, -ere, -dūxī, -ductum (*v.t.*): lead through, bring, bring over.

peregrīnātiō, -ōnis (*f.*): living abroad.

perferō, -ferre, -tulī, -lātum (*v.t.*): endure, carry.

perficiō, -ere, -fēcī, -fectum (*v.t.*): complete.

perfugiō, -ere, -fūgī (*v.i.*): flee.

perīculum, -ī (*n.*): danger.

perillustris, -e: very notable.

perpetuō (*adv.*): constantly, always.

perpetuus, -a, -um: permanent.

perscrībō, -ere, -scrīpsī, -scrīptum (*v.t.*): write in full.

persequor, -ī, -secūtus sum (*v.t.*): follow after, go through, proceed against.

persuādeō, -ēre, -sī, -sum (*v.i.* with *dat.*): persuade.

pertaedet, -ēre, -taesum est (*impers. vb.*): it wearies (with *acc.* of person, *gen.* of cause).

perterreō, -ēre, -uī, -itum (*v.t.*): thoroughly frighten.

pertimeō, -ēre, -uī (*v.t.*): fear greatly, be thoroughly afraid.

pertineō, -ēre, -uī, -tentum (*v.i.*): pertain, extend; **pertinere ad:** be connected with.

perturbō, -āre, -āvī, -ātum (*v.t.*): thoroughly disturb.

pervehō, -ere, -vexī, -vectum (*v.t.*): carry; (*pass.*) travel.

perveniō, -īre, -vēnī, -ventum (*v.i.*): come to, arrive.

petō, -ere, -īvī and -iī, -ītum (*v.t.*): seek, ask.

philosophia, -ae (*f.*): philosophy.

philosophus, -ī (*m.*): philosopher.

pietās, -ātis (*f.*): sense of duty.

pīla, -ae (*f.*): pillar.

plēbs, plēbis (*f.*): people, the masses.

plēctō, -ere (*v.t.*): beat, flog.

plēnus, -a, -um (with *gen.*): full.

plērīque, plēraeque, plēraque: most.

plērumque (*adv.*): for the most part.

plūrimus, -a, -um (*sup. adj.*): most, very many.

plūs, plūris: more; (*adv.*) **plūs, plūrimum:** more, most.

poēma, -atis (*n.*): poem.

poēta, -ae (*c.*): poet.

poēticē, -ēs (*f.*): poetry.

poēticus, -a, -um: concerning poetry, poetic.

polliceor, -ērī, -itus sum (*v.i.* and *t.*): promise.

pompa, -ae (*f.*): procession.

pōnō, -ere, posuī, positum (*v.t.*): put, place, set up.

populus, -ī (*m.*): people.

porrigō, -ere, -rēxī, -rēctum (*v.t.*): stretch out.

portus, -ūs (*m.*): harbour.

poscō, -ere, poposcī (*v.t.*): demand.

possessiō, -ōnis (*f.*): possession.

possum, posse, potuī (*v.i.*): be able, be powerful.

post (*adv.* and *prep.* with *acc.*): after; **post ... quam:** after.

posteā (*adv.*): afterwards; **postea ... quam:** after (*conj.*).

posteāquam, postquam (*conj.*): after.

postulō, -āre, -āvī, -ātum (*v.t.*): demand.

potēns, -entis: powerful.

potentia, -ae (*f.*): power.

potestās, -ātis (*f.*): power, opportunity.

potior, potīrī, potītus sum (*v.i.* with *gen.* or *abl.*): gain control of.

potior, -ius (*comp. adj.*): preferable.

potissimum (*sup. adv.*): especially, above all others.

potius (*comp. adv.*): rather.

praebeō, -ēre, -uī, -itum (*v.t.*): show, provide.

praeceptum, -ī (*n.*): instruction.

praecipitō, -āre, -āvī, -ātum (*v.t.*): throw headlong.

praecipuē (*adv.*): outstandingly, especially.

praecipuus, -a, -um: outstanding.

praeda, -ae (*f.*): booty.

praedīcō, -āre, -āvī, -ātum (*v.t.*): state publicly, declare.

praedīcō, -ere, -dīxī, -dictum (*v.t.*): foretell.

praedium, -iī (*n.*): estate.

praedor, -ārī, -ātus sum (*v.t.*): plunder.

praefectūra, -ae (*f.*): administrative position.

praefectus, -ī (*m.*): commander, governor.

praeficiō, -ere, -fēcī, -fectum (*v.t.*): place in command.

praemium, -iī (*n.*): reward.

praeoccupō, -āre, -āvī, -ātum (*v.t.*): attack first.

praeoptō, -āre, -āvī, -ātum (*v.t.*): prefer.

praes, praedis (*m.*): guarantor.

praescrībō, -ere, -scrīpsi, -scrīptum (*v.t.*): prescribe, direct.

praesēns, -entis: present, in person; **in praesenti**: for the present, at the time; **in praesentia**: on the spot.

praesertim (*adv.*): especially.

praesidium, -iī (*n.*): garrison, protection.

praestāns, -antis: outstanding.

praestō, -āre, -stitī, -stitum (*v.t.* and *i.*): provide, surpass.

praesum, -esse, -fuī (*v.i.* and with *dat.*): be present, be in charge of.

praeter (*prep.* with *acc.*): except, besides.

praetereā (*adv.*): besides.

praetereō, -īre, -iī, -itum (*v.t.*): pass over.

praeterquam (*adv.*): other than, except, beyond.

praetor, -ōris (*m.*): praetor, commander, general.

praetōrius, -iī (*m.*): ex-praetor.

precēs, -um (*f. pl.*): prayers.

pretiōsus, -a, -um: valuable, costly.

pretium, -iī (*n.*): price, cost.

pridiē (*adv.*): on the day before.

prīmum (*adv.*): first, firstly.

prīmus, -a, -um: first; **in prīmīs**: among the first, especially.

princeps, -cipis: first, leading; (*subst.*) leader.

principātus, -ūs (*m.*): leadership.

prior, prius (*comp. adj.*): earlier, former.

pristinus, -a, -um: former, previous.

priusquam, prius . . . quam (*conj.*): before.

prīvātus, -a, -um: private.

prīvignus, -ī (*m.*): stepson.

prō (*prep.* with *abl.*): for, instead of, in accordance with.

probō, -āre, -āvī, -ātum (*v.t.*): approve.

procella, -ae (*f.*): storm.

prōcreō, -āre, -āvī, -ātum (*v.t.*): beget.

prōcūrātiō, -ōnis (*f.*): administration, undertaking.

prōcūrō, -āre, -āvī, -ātum (*v.t.*): look after.

prōdeō, -īre, -iī, -itum (*v.i.*): go forward, come out.

prōdō, -ere, -didī, -ditum (*v.t.*): hand down, betray.

prōdūcō, -ere, -dūxī, -ductum (*v.t.*): prolong, extend.

proelium, -iī (*n.*): battle.

prōficiō, -ere, -fēcī, -fectum (*v.i.*): make progress, advance, improve.

proficiscor, -ī, profectus sum (*v.i.*): set out, proceed.

prōfugiō, -ere, -fugī (*v.i.*): flee (esp. into exile).

prohibeō, -ēre, -uī, -itum (*v.t.*): prevent.

proinde (*adv.*): just so, in the same way; **proinde . . . ac**: just as.

prōlābor, -ī, -lapsus sum
(v.i.): collapse.

prōmittō, -ere, -mīsī, -mis-
sum (v.t.): promise.

prōnuntiō, -āre, -āvī, -ātum
(v.t.): recite.

propāgō, -inis (f.): offspring,
descendant.

prope (adv.): nearly.

propinquitās, -ātis (f.): relationship.

prōpōnō, -ere, -posuī, -posi-
tum (v.t.): put before, pro-
pose.

prōpositum, -ī (n.): intention.

proprius, -a, -um: one's own,
personal.

propter (prep. with acc.): on
account of.

prōrumpō, -ere, -rūpī, -rup-
tum (v.i.): burst out.

prōscrībō, -ere, -scrīpsī,
-scrīptum (v.t.): proscribe.

prōscrīptiō, -ōnis (f.): proscription.

prōsequor, -ī, -secūtus sum
(v.t.): accompany.

prosper, -era, -erum: according to one's hopes, successful.

prosperē (adv.): successfully.

prosperitās, -ātis (f.): success,
good fortune.

prōsum, prōdesse, prōfuī
(v.i. with dat.): be a help.

prōut (adv.): just as.

prōvincia, -ae (f.): sphere of
office, province.

prūdēns, -entis: prudent, sens-
ible.

prūdentia, -ae (f.): foresight,
prudence.

pūbes, -eris: grown up, adult.

pūblicē (adv.): publicly, by the
state, from public funds.

pūblicō, -āre, -āvī, -ātum
(v.t.): make public, confiscate.

pūblicus, -a, -um: public.

puer, -erī (m.): boy, slave.

puerīlis, -e: of a boy.

pueritia, -ae (f.): boyhocd.

pulchrē (adv.): beautifully.

pūs, pūris (n.): pus, matter.

putō, -āre, -āvī, -ātum (v.t.):
think, suppose.

Q: Quintus (Roman praenomen).

quaerō, -ere, quaesīvī, quae-
sītum (v.t.): seek, ask.

quaestiō, -ōnis (f.): enquiry,
question, trial.

quaestus, -ūs (m.): gain,
profit.

quālis, -e: what sort of; quālis
... tālis: such ... as.

quam (adv.): how, as, than.

quamdiū (conj.): how long, as
long as.

quamquam (conj.): although.

quamvīs (conj.): however
much, although.

quantus, -a, -um: how great,
how much, as great, as much.

quārē (adv.): wherefore, why.

quartus, -a, -um: fourth.

quaternī, -ae, -a: four each.

-que (enclitic conj.): and.

quemadmodum (adv.): how.

queō, -īre, -īvī and -iī, -itum
(v.i.): be able.

querimōnia, -ae (f.): com-
plaint.

quī, quae, quod (rel. pron.):
who, which.

quīcumque, quaecumque,
quodcumque (rel. pron.):
whoever, whatever.

quid (adv.): why.

quīdam, quaedam, quod-
dam: a certain; (pl.) some.

quidem (adv.): indeed; ne
... quidem: not even.

quiēs, -ētis (*f.*): quiet, neutrality.

quiēscō, -ere, quiēvī, quiētum (*v.i.*): grow quiet, be quiet, sleep.

quīn (*conj.*): but that, without; (*adv.*) indeed; quīn etiam: what is more.

quīngentī, -ae, -a: 500.

quīnī, -ae, -a: five each.

quīnquāgēnī, -ae, -a: fifty each.

quīnquāgintā: fifty.

quīnque: five.

quīntus, -a, -um: fifth.

quippe (*adv.* and *conj.*): certainly, inasmuch as.

quis, quid (*interrog. pron.*): who, what.

quis, qua, quid (*indef. pron.*): any one, any (after *si, ne, nisi, num*).

quisquam, quaequam, quicquam (*indef. pron.*): anyone, anything.

quisque, quaeque, quodque (*indef. pron.*): each, every.

quisquis, quaequae, quodquod and quicquid (*rel. adj.* and *pron.*): whoever, whatever.

quīvīs, quaevīs, quodvīs and quidvīs (*indef. adj.* and *pron.*): anyone you like, anything whatever.

quō (*adv.*): whither; so that, in order that.

quoad (*adv.*): so far as, so long as.

quod (*conj.*): because, that.

quodsī (*conj.*): now if.

quoniam (*conj.*): because.

quōquam (*adv.*): to any place.

quoque (*conj.*): also.

quōrsum (*adv.*): whither.

quotiēnscumque (*adv.*): whenever, as often as.

ratiō, -ōnis (*f.*): method. reason.

ratus, -a, -um: valid.

recēdō, -ere, -cessī, -cessum (*v.i.*): depart, retire.

recidō, -ere, -cidī, -cāsum (*v.i.*): fall again.

recipiō, -ere, -cēpī, -ceptum (*v.t.*): take back, recover.

reconciliō, -āre, -āvī, -ātum (*v.t.*): reconcile, make friendly.

recumbō, -ere, -cubuī (*v.i.*): recline.

recuperō, -āre, -āvī, -ātum (*v.t.*): recover.

reddō, -ere, -didī, -ditum (*v.t.*): give back, render, make.

redeō, -īre, -iī, -itum (*v.i.*): go back, return.

redimō, -ere, -ēmī, -emptum (*v.t.*): buy back, ransom, rescue.

reditus, -ūs (*m.*): return, restoration, income.

redūcō, -ere, -dūxī, -ductum (*v.t.*): bring back, take back.

referō, -ferre, rettulī, relātum (*v.t.*): bring back, relate, quote, set down in writing.

reficiō, -ere, -fēcī, -fectum (*v.t.*): remake, repair.

rēgius, -a, -um: of a king.

rēgnum, -ī (*n.*): kingdom.

rēligiō, -ōnis (*f.*): religious scruple, religion.

rēligiōsē (*adv.*): scrupulously.

relinquō, -ere, -līquī, -lictum (*v.t.*): leave, abandon.

reliquus, -a, -um: remaining, rest.

remaneō, -ēre, -mansī (*v.i.*): remain.

remedium, -iī (*n.*): remedy.

rēmex, -igis (*m.*): rower.

remigrō, -āre, -āvī, -ātum (*v.i.*): return.

reminīscor, -ī (*v.t.*): call to mind, imagine.

remittō, -ere, -mīsī, -missum (*v.t.*): send back, restore from exile, relax.

removeō, -ēre, -mōvī, -mōtum (*v.t.*): remove.

renūntiō, -āre, -āvī, -ātum (*v.t.*): renounce.

reor, rērī, ratus sum (*v.t.*): think.

repentīnus, -a, -um: sudden, unforeseen.

reperiō, -īre, repperī, repertum (*v.t.*): find.

reprehendō, -ere, -dī, -sum (*v.t.*): rebuke, blame.

reprimō, -ere, -pressī, -pressum (*v.t.*): repress, crush.

repugnō, -are, -āvī, -ātum (*v.i.* with *dat.*): fight against, be opposed to.

reputō, -āre, -āvī, -ātum (*v.t.*): think over.

requīrō, -ere, -sīvī, -sītum (*v.t.*): ask, inquire.

rēs, rēī (*f.*): thing, property, circumstance; **res gestae:** achievements; **res publica:** state, public life.

resacrō, -āre, -āvī, -ātum (*v.t.*): remove a curse from.

reservō, -āre, -āvī, -ātum (*v.t.*): keep back, save.

resistō, -ere, -stitī (*v.i.* with *dat.*): resist.

restituō, -ere, -uī, -ūtum (*v.t.*): restore.

retineō, -ēre, -uī, -tentum (*v.t.*): retain, preserve.

reus, -ī (*m.*): defendant.

revertor, -ī, -versus sum (*v.i.*): turn back, return.

revocō, -āre, -āvī, -ātum (*v.t.*): recall.

rēx, rēgis (*m.*): king.

rhapsōdia, -ae (*f.*): epic poem, book of Homer's *Iliad*.

rōbustus, -a, -um: strong, sturdy.

rogātus, -ūs (*m.*): request.

rogō, -āre, -āvī, -ātum (*v.t.*): ask.

rūmor, -ōris (*m.*): rumour.

rūrsus (*adv.*): again.

rūsticus, -a, -um: in the country, rustic.

sacer, -cra, -crum: sacred; **sacra** (*n. pl.*): sacred rites.

sacerdōs, -dōtis (*c.*): priest.

sacrilegium, -iī (*n.*): sacrilege.

saepe (*adv.*): often.

saepiō, -īre, -psī, -ptum (*v.t.*): surround.

sagācitās, -ātis (*f.*): shrewdness.

sal, -is (*m.*): salt, good taste, wit.

salūs, -ūtis (*f.*): safety, wellbeing, health.

salutāris, -e: health-giving, beneficial.

salvus, -a, -um: safe.

sānciō, -īre, -nxī, -nctum (*v.t.*): consecrate, confirm.

sānctus, -a, -um: holy.

sanguis, -inis (*m.*): blood.

sānō, -āre, -āvī, -ātum (*v.t.*): heal, cure.

sapientia, -ae (*f.*): wisdom.

satis (*adv.*): sufficiently.

satisfaciō, -ere, -fēcī, -factum (*v.i.* with *dat.*): satisfy.

satrapēs, -is (*m.*): satrap (a Persian governor).

scelerātus, -a, -um: wicked, criminal.

sciō, scīre, scīvī, scītum (*v.t.*): know.

scītum, -ī (*n.*): vote, decision.

scopulōsus, -a, -um: full of rocks.

scrībō, -ere, scrīpsī, scrīptum (*v.t.*): write.

sē, sēsē: himself, themselves, etc.

secundus, -a, -um: following, second, favourable, successful.

secus (*adv.*): differently, otherwise; **secus ac:** otherwise than.

sed (*conj.*): but.

sēdō, -āre, -āvī, -ātum (*v.t.*): settle, calm.

sēiungō, -ere, -iunxī, -iunctum (*v.t.*): separate.

semel (*adv.*): once.

senectūs, -tūtis (*f.*): old age.

senēscō, -ere, senuī (*v.i.*): grow old, decline.

senex, -is (*m.*): old man.

sēnsim (*adv.*): gently, gradually.

sēnsus, -ūs (*m.*): feeling, view.

sententia, -ae (*f.*): opinion, maxim, expectation.

sentiō, -īre, sēnsī, sēnsum (*v.t.*): feel, realise.

sēparātim (*adv.*): separately.

sepeliō, -īre, -īvī and **-iī, sepultum** (*v.t.*): bury.

septem: seven.

sepulcrum, -ī (*n.*): tomb.

sequor, -ī, secūtus sum (*v.t.*): follow.

sermō, -mōnis (*m.*): conversation.

serviō, -īre, -īvī and **-iī, -ītum** (*v.i.* with *dat.*): serve, be subject to, have regard for.

servō, -āre, -āvī, -ātum (*v.t.*): save.

sestertius, -iī, *gen. pl.* **-ium** (*m.*): sesterce (a small silver coin).

sētius (*comp. adv.*): differently, otherwise.

sevēritās, -ātis (*f.*): strictness.

sexāgintā: sixty.

sī (*conj.*): if.

sīc (*adv.*): thus, so.

sīcut (*adv.*): just as.

sīgnificō, -āre, -āvī, -ātum (*v.t.*): indicate.

sīgnum, -ī (*n.*): sign, indication.

silva, -ae (*f.*): wood, forest.

similis, -e (with *gen.* or *dat.*): similar, like.

similitūdō, -inis (*f.*): likeness.

simul (*adv.*): together; **simul atque:** as soon as; **simul cum:** at the same time as.

simulō, -āre, -āvī, -ātum (*v.t.*): pretend.

simultās, -ātis (*f.*): rivalry, feud.

sine (*prep.* with *abl.*): without.

singulāris, -e: single, sole, exclusive, remarkable, unique.

singulī, -ae, -a: one each, single, each one.

sistō, -ere, stitī (*v.t.*): make to stand; **vadimonium sistere:** appear in court after bail has been given.

situs, -a, -um: situated.

sōbrius, -a, -um: sober.

socer, -erī (*m.*): father-in-law.

sociētās, -ātis (*f.*): alliance, association, sharing.

socius, -iī (*m.*): ally, accomplice.

soleō, -ēre, solitus sum (*v.i.*): be accustomed.

sōlum (*adv.*): only.

sōlus, -a, -um: alone.

somnus, -ī (*m.*): sleep.

sonitus, -ūs (*m.*): sound.
sōpiō, -īre, -īvī and -iī, -ītum (*v.t.*): lull to sleep.
sopor, -ōris (*m.*): sleep, sleeping draught.
soror, -ōris (*f.*): sister.
specimen, -minis (*n.*): sign, indication.
speculātor, -ōris (*m.*): scout, spy.
spērō, -āre, -āvī, -ātum (*v.t.*): hope, hope for.
spēs, speī (*f.*): hope.
spīritus, -ūs (*m.*): breath, spirit.
splendidē (*adv.*): with distinction.
splendidus, -a, -um: magnificent, distinguished.
splendor, -ōris (*m.*): magnificence.
spoliō, -āre, -āvī, -ātum (*v.t.*): strip, rob.
spondeō, -ēre, spopondī, spōnsum (*v.t.*): promise, pledge.
spōnsālia, -ium (*n. pl.*): betrothal, engagement.
spōnsor, -ōris (*m.*): bondsman, surety.
statua, -ae (*f.*): statue.
statuō, -ere, -uī, -ūtum (*v.t.*): decide, arrange.
status, -ūs (*m.*): state, condition.
stipulātiō, -ōnis (*f.*): agreement, covenant.
stirps, -pis (*f.*): stock, origin.
stō, -āre, stetī, statum (*v.i.*): stand.
strepitus, -ūs (*m.*): din.
studeō, -ēre, -uī (*v.i. and t.*): be eager, desire.
studium, -iī (*n.*): eagerness, enthusiasm, desire, rivalry.

studiōsus, -a, -um: zealous; (with *gen.*): fond of.
suāvitās, -ātis (*f.*): pleasantness, charm.
sub (*prep.* with *abl.*): under, during; (with *acc.*) just before.
subālāris, -e: carried under the arm.
subdūcō, -ere, -dūxī, -ductum (*v.t.*): remove secretly.
subitō (*adv.*): suddenly.
subitus, -a, -um: sudden.
sublevō, -āre, -āvī, -ātum (*v.t.*): lighten, support.
subscrībō, -ere, -scrīpsī, -scrīptum (*v.t.*): sign beneath.
substituō, -ere, -uī, -ūtum (*v.t.*): substitute.
subsum, -esse (*v.i.*): be under, underlie.
subtexō, -ere, -uī, -tum (*v.t.*): weave under, add.
suburbānus, -a, -um: near the city.
succēdō, -ere, -cessī, -cessum (*v.i. with dat.*): follow.
succendō, -ere, -dī, -cēnsum (*v.t.*): set on fire (from below).
succurrō, -ere, -currī, -cursum (*v.i. with dat.*): run to help.
suffrāgor, -ārī, -ātus sum (*v.i.*): ask for votes, canvass.
sum, esse, fuī: be.
summus, -a, -um: highest, greatest, most distinguished.
sūmō, -ere, sumpsī, sumptum (*v.t.*): take, consume.
sumptus, -ūs (*m.*): expense.
sumptuōsus, -a, -um: extravagant, expensive.
supellex, supellectilis (*f.*): furniture.
superior, -ius (*comp. adj.*): upper, stronger, earlier.

superō, -āre, -āvī, -ātum (*v.t.*): overcome, surpass.

superstes, -stitis: surviving, survivor.

supersum or **super sum, esse, fuī** (*v.i.*): be left, survive.

suppeditō, -āre, -āvī, -ātum (*v.t.*): supply.

suppetō, -ere, -īvī, -ītum (*v.i.*): be at hand, be available.

supportō, -āre, -āvī, -ātum (*v.t.*): carry.

suprā (*adv.* and *prep.* with *acc.*): above, higher, beyond.

suprēmus, -a, -um (*sup. adj.*): last.

surgō, -ere, surrēxī, surrēctum (*v.i.*): arise.

suscipiō, -ere, -cēpī, -ceptum (*v.t.*): undertake.

suspiciō, -ere, -spēxī, -spectum (*v.t.*): look up to, respect.

suspiciō, -ōnis (*f.*): suspicion.

suus, -a, -um: his own, their own, etc.

T.: Titus (Roman *praenomen*).

taceō, -ēre, -uī, -itum (*v.i.*): be silent, remain silent.

taciturnus, -a, -um: silent.

talentum, -ī (*n.*): talent.

tālis, -e: such; **tālis ... quālis:** such ... as.

tam (*adv.*): so.

tamen (*adv.*): yet, nevertheless.

tantopere (*adv.*): so much.

tantum (*adv.*): only, merely.

tantus, -a, -um: so great, so large.

tectum, -ī (*n.*): roof, house.

tegō, -ere, texī, tectum (*v.t.*): cover, protect.

tēlum, -ī (*n.*): javelin, weapon.

temerē (*adv.*): carelessly, rashly.

tempestās, -ātis (*f.*): storm.

temporārius, -a, -um: depending on circumstances.

tempus, -oris (*n.*): time, opportunity.

teneō, -ēre, -uī, -tum (*v.t.*): hold.

tēnesmos, -ī (*m.*): straining, constipation.

tentō, -āre, -āvī, -ātum (*v.t.*): attempt.

ternī, -ae, -a: three each, three.

terra, -ae (*f.*): land.

terrestris, -e: land.

terror, -ōris (*m.*): terror, fear.

tertius, -a, -um: third.

testāmentum, -ī (*n.*): will.

testātus, -a, -um: public, well known.

testimōnium, -iī (*n.*): evidence.

testis, -is (*c.*): witness.

Ti.: Tiberius (Roman *praenomen*).

timeō, -ēre, -uī (*v.t.*): fear.

timor, -ōris (*m.*): fear.

tollō, -ere, sustulī, sublātum (*v.t.*): remove, destroy.

tot (*indecl. adj.*): so many.

totidem (*indecl. adj.*): the same number of.

tōtus, -a, -um: whole.

trādō, -ere, -didī, -ditum (*v.t.*): hand over.

trāiciō, -ere, -iēcī, -iectum (*v.t.*): send across, transfer.

tranquillō, -āre, -āvī, -ātum (*v.t.*): calm.

tranquillitās, -ātis (*f.*): peace of mind.

transeō, -īre, -iī, -itum (*v.i.* and *t.*): cross, go across.

trēcentī, -ae, -a: 300.

trēs, tria: three.

tribūnus, -ī (*m.*): tribune.

tribuō, -ere, -uī, -ūtum (v.t.):
assign, bestow.
triēris, -is (f.): trireme.
trigintā: thirty.
trirēmis, -is (f.): trireme.
triticum, -ī (n.): wheat.
triumvir, -ī (m.): triumvir,
member of a board of three.
tū: you (sing.).
tueor, -ērī, tuitus sum (v.t.):
watch, look after.
tum (adv.): then; cum . . .
tum: not only . . . but also,
both . . . and.
tumultus, -ūs (m.): disorder.
turpis, -e: disgraceful.
tūtēla, -ae (f.): protection.
tūtus, -a, -um: safe.
tyrānnis, -idis (f.): tyranny,
monarchy.
tyrānnus, -ī (m.): tyrant,
monarch.
ubi (conj.): when, where.
ubinam (conj.): where.
ulcīscor, -ī, ultus sum (v.t.):
avenge.
ūllus, -a, -um: any.
ūltimus, -a, -um (sup. adj.):
last, furthest.
umquam (adv.): ever.
ūniversus, -a, -um: entire, all.
ūnus, -a, -um: one, alone.
urbānus, -a, -um: of the city,
in the city.
urbs, -bis (f.): city.
usque (adv.): even, quite;
usque ad: right up to;
usque eo: to such an extent.
ūsūra, -ae (f.): interest.
ūsus, -ūs (m.): use, usefulness,
familiarity, experience; usu
venire: happen.
ut (adv. and conj.): how, as,
when, in order that, so that.
uter, utra, utrum: which of
two.

uterque, utraque, utrumque:
each (of two), both.
ūtilis, -e: useful, expedient.
ūtilitās, -ātis (f.): usefulness,
expediency.
ūtor, -ī, ūsus sum (v.i. with
abl.): use, treat, have, enjoy.
utrum (conj.): whether; utrum
. . . an: whether . . . or.
uxor, uxōris (f.): wife.

vacātiō, -ōnis (f.): exemption
from military service.
vadimōnium, -iī (n.): bail,
security, surety.
valeō, -ēre, -uī (v.i.): be
strong, be effective.
valetūdō, -inis (f.): health.
varietās, -ātis (f.): variation.
vātēs, -is (c.): seer, prophet.
vectīgal, -ālis (n.): tax, re-
venue.
vel (conj.): or; vel . . . vel:
either . . . or.
venditō, -āre, -āvī, -ātum
(v.t.): sell.
venerius, -a, -um: belonging
to Venus (goddess of love).
venia, -ae (f.): indulgence,
favour.
veniō, -īre, vēnī ventum
(v.i.): come.
vēnor, -ārī, -ātus sum (v.i.
and t.): hunt.
venter, -tris (m.): stomach.
ventitō, -āre, -āvī, -ātum
(v.i.): come repeatedly.
vēnumdo, -dare, -dedī, -da-
tum (v.t.): sell into slavery.
verbum, -ī (n.): word.
verbōsus, -a, -um: wordy,
long-winded.
vērē (adv.): truly.
vereor, -ērī, veritus sum
(v.t.): fear, respect.
vērō (adv.): but, indeed.

versor, -ārī, -ātus sum (*v.i.*): go to and fro, busy oneself.

versūra, -ae (*f.*): loan.

versus, -us (*m.*): verse, line.

vestimentum, -ī (*n.*): clothing.

vestis, -is (*f.*): clothing.

vetus, -eris: old.

vetustās, -ātis (*f.*): age.

vexō, -āre, -āvī, -ātum (*v.t.*): harass.

vīciēns (*adv.*): twenty times.

vīcīnitās, -ātis (*f.*): neighbourhood.

victor, -ōris (*m.*): victor; (*adj.*) victorious.

victōria, -ae (*f.*): victory.

victus, -ūs (*m.*): way of life.

videō, -ēre, vīdī, vīsum (*v.t.*): see; (*pass.*): seem.

vigeō, -ēre, -uī (*v.i.*): flourish, thrive.

villa, -ae (*f.*): country house.

vincō, -ere, vīcī, victum (*v.t.*): conquer, surpass.

vīnolentus, -a, -um: fond of wine.

vīnum, -ī (*n.*): wine.

violō, -āre, -āvī, -ātum (*v.t.*): violate, maltreat.

vir, virī (*m.*): man.

virgō, -inis (*f.*): maiden.

virtūs, -ūtis (*f.*): manliness, courage, virtue, ability.

vīs, vim, vī (*f.*): violence; *pl.* **vīrēs**: strength.

vīsō, -ere, vīsī, vīsum (*v.t.*): see, survey.

vīta, -ae (*f.*): life.

vitium, -iī (*n.*): fault, vice, mistake.

vītō, -āre, -āvī, -ātum (*v.t.*): avoid.

vīvo, -ere, vīxī vīctum (*v.i.*): live.

vīvus, -a, -um: alive.

vix (*adv.*): scarcely.

vocitō, -āre, -āvī, -ātum (*v.t.*): call.

vocō, -āre, -āvī, -atum (*v.t.*): call, invite.

volō, velle, voluī (*v.t. and i.*): wish, be willing.

volūmen, -minis (*n.*): roll, volume.

voluntās, -ātis (*f.*): wish, willingness, good will, attitude.

vōs: you (*pl.*).

vōx, vōcis (*f.*): voice.

vulgus, -ī (*n.*): crowd, common people, the public; **vulgo** (*adv.*): everywhere.

vulnus, -eris (*n.*): wound.

vultus, -ūs (*m.*): countenance, features.